MICHAEL J. BIELAWA

THE
History
PRESS

Published by The History Press
Charleston, SC 29403
www.historypress.net

Copyright © 2013 by Michael J. Bielawa
All rights reserved

*Front cover, top*: Sheet music cover for *Carbarlick Acid Rag. Composed by Clarence C. Wiley, 1905.*
*Bottom*: "Plan of New Haven." *Courtesy Library of Congress Geography and Map Division. Clockwise from top left*: Schooner *Robert P. King, copyright Mystic Seaport, Mystic, Connecticut, #1976.1.171.12;*
the prophetess Rhoda Wakeman, *from the Collection of the Sterling and Francine Clark Art Institute Library, Williamstown, Massachusetts;* Czar Nicholas II, *courtesy of the Michael J. Bielawa Collection;* "Modern Demoniacs," *from J.W. Daniels, Spiritualism Versus Christianity.*
*Back cover, top*: Devils drumming over building, *from Joseph Glanvill,* Saducismus triumphatus.
*Top left*: Sperry Lighthouse. *Courtesy of the Michael J. Bielawa Collection. Center*: Witches gathering with Satan, *from Glanvill,* Saducismus triumphatus. *Bottom*: West side of East Rock, from *John Warner Barber,* History and Antiquities of New Haven. *Courtesy of the New Haven Museum Photo Archives.*

First published 2013

Manufactured in the United States

ISBN 978.1.60949.889.4

Library of Congress CIP data applied for.

*Notice*: The information in this book is true and complete to the best of our knowledge. It is offered without guarantee on the part of the author or The History Press. The author and The History Press disclaim all liability in connection with the use of this book.

*"Is this Hell?" the boy asked.*
*"No son," his father replied...*
*"It is only New Haven."*

*New Haven Museum, Display Description*
*Chapel Street Railroad Station*
*1849*

# Contents

# Acknowledgements

O ne of the most satisfying aspects of preparing any history—and, in this case, a very wicked history—entails the romantic pursuit associated with research. The most fundamental expedition, sans pith helmet, requires traveling to museums, historical societies and libraries and especially interviewing the fascinating individuals dedicated to preserving the unique New Haven we all share. Realms gathered on bookshelves, hidden in reels of microfilm and revealed in forgotten memories are real treasure maps. As investigation deemed necessary, and Yankee luck dictated, I was led to the four corners of southern New England: north to the Vermont border, east to outside of Boston, south to the Mystic shore and west into Fairfield County, Connecticut (actually even beyond these to the borough of Brooklyn's tall ships and their jack-tars). But the Elm City naturally provided the compass's unwavering center. *Wicked New Haven* came into being with the assistance of dynamic institutions, organizations and eager individuals.

I wish to thank the following: the docks and narrow lanes of Mystic Seaport: the Museum of America and the Sea leads not only to yesterday but to history's future; its incredible Collections Research Center and Louisa Alger Watrous, whose help brought the photograph of the *Robert P. King* onto these pages; Libby Oldham, research associate and copy editor at the Nantucket Historical Association Research Library—I enjoyed each of our illuminating conversations about the schooner *Robert P. King* and the strange travels of the vessel's quarterboard; the Brooklyn Historical Society, the Othmer Library and Jacob Nadal, director of the library and archives;

collections access and reference librarian Karen Bucky at the Sterling and Francine Clark Art Institute Library in Williamstown, Massachusetts (where you can pace the history of the French and Indian War and stare down gigantic glowing eyeballs); all the friendly and helpful folks at the American Antiquarian Society in Worcester, Massachusetts—everyone who enters this palace of print is made to feel like a king; the Connecticut State Library and some of our region's greatest resources, namely, wonderful state librarian Kendall Wiggin and librarians Mel Smith, Jeannie Sherman and Mr. Energy personified, Kevin Johnson of the history and genealogy department—you are each a source of Nutmeg inspiration; the New Haven Museum executive director Margaret Anne Tockarshewsky supported this project from its inception, director of photographic archives Jason Bischoff-Wurstle happily helped track down a number of rare images, the staff at the museum's outstanding Whitney Library—Bonnie Campbell, James Campbell, Edward Surato and Frances Skelton—shared knowledge and kindness, Donna Wardle cemented my acquiring fantastic photographs from the New Haven Museum's collection, and Bill McDonald, my old friend from the *Connecticut Post*, greeted me every Friday I passed through the museum's front doors; Florence Gillich, at Yale University's Historical Library, Cushing/Whitney Medical Library—you are a pleasure to know, and the Yale campus and those grinning gargoyles continue to empower the imagination; and Ewa Wolynska of the Elihu Burritt Library at Central Connecticut State University—thanks for helping my brother, Matthew, come in contact with the haunted essence of Cotton Mather's three-hundred-year-old tome. (This brings me to some of *Wicked New Haven*'s good New England gris-gris: one late night, my writing was taking a turn for the slower. I was stumped about the process of the founding and union of West Haven and Orange, Connecticut. I gave Matt, who lives way up in Newington, a call, just to remove the funk. To our mutual surprise, my brother happened to be avoiding a midnight traffic tie-up on I-95 and was driving in downtown West Haven—right in front of the city's historical marker. Thanks, Matt, for declouding the bulky facts I'd tripped over.)

I also want to thank David J. DeRubeis, managing partner and funeral director of the Cody-White Funeral Home in downtown Milford, Connecticut, who, with the help of the state library and the Museum of Connecticut History, helped me track down a painting of Governor Charles Hobby Pond, of which an excellent rendition now adorns the Ponds' old home and this book. The funeral parlor is located in a Greek Revival–style home built in 1845 by the family of Governor Pond.

Additional gratitude goes to Tim Harrison, editor of *Lighthouse Digest*, for sharing his beautiful publication; Anna J. Cook, reference librarian at the Massachusetts Historical Society; Mary Witkowski at the Bridgeport Public Library History Center and this institution's incredible databases and newspaper collections; Fairfield University's DiMenna-Nyselius Library; the Ives Main Branch of the New Haven Free Public Library and local history librarian Allison Botelho, librarian Tom Smith and all those brave New Haven–library souls who each Halloween-time gather to raise a glass to the memory of Evergreen Cemetery's most famous resident, "Midnight Mary"; and the Library of Congress director for preservation, J. Mark Sweeney, who happily grabbed hold of a shovel when an old grave (illustration) needed digging. Working with Jeff Saraceno and the keen eye of Julia Turner enhanced and made enjoyable the entire editorial process.

I want to also thank the ring of strategically located New Haven County coffeehouses, where I composed much of these pages, for their relaxing hospitality, treats and torts: New Haven's Koffee on Audubon, Panera Bread and Starbucks in Southbury and the late-night fireside in Middlebury's Dunkin' Donuts.

And, finally, I thank brother writer Andre Dubus III (forgive me for starting a sentence with *and*), who on an early spring day shared a little Faulkner, Flaubert and Hemingway and a lot of much needed laughter.

# A Brief Treatise on the Reality of Yesterday and Thus the Existence of the Known and Unknown in New England

*From what I hear, there is no doubt that something will allow itself to be seen or to be heard—something perhaps, excessively horrible. Do you think, if I take you with me, I may rely on your presence of mind, whatever may happen?*
—*Lord Edward Bulwer-Lytton*

New Haven has been blessed with an exuberant and complex history. Luckily, its story has been possessed by outstanding historians. Insightful books and essays will always continue to bubble forth, churning and interpreting this region's multifaceted geology, prehistory and Puritan founding as well as its maritime, industrial, immigrant and riotous past. Another aspect of New Haven's fascinating and evolving narrative lurks in peculiar shadows, however, and deserves concise exploration: the waking dream of this city's paranormal. Like an unhinged and deteriorating leather-bound book or a steel canister full of disintegrating celluloid, the strange events and personalities, once enrapturing olden Connecticut, are in danger of being lost. *Wicked New Haven* seeks to preserve, and share, a sampling of these brittle mementos. Each of these stories is firmly rooted in our historic record, as much as parchment deeds and gravestones.

There is precedent in such a history being collated found, over the centuries, in tales and poetry of New Haven's "Phantom Ship" and the examination of court documents concerning local witch trials. Recent incantations include the frightful retellings of Evergreen Cemetery's most infamous resident,

"Midnight Mary." But like Center Church's surreal underground crypt, there is a much deeper realm of the weird quivering at New Haven's core. Such a postmodern chronicle should be considered an embrace or homage to those Octoberesque New England tracts, of Increase and Cotton Mather, focusing on wonders and the invisible.

Writing about New Haven history is like poking a fire. The littlest toe kick (that is, pen nudge) can conjure a rippling illumination. Embers buried deepest in that glow, like forgotten memories suddenly emblazoned, hold the most beguiling heat. The realities of this coastal community, like all of Connecticut, smolder in those way-down, hidden layers. New England's consuming legends, hauntings and bizarre crimes silently bide their time, waiting to reignite from this strata of darkest spark. *Wicked New Haven* takes hold of a fireside poker and thrashes these blood-red coals. Inspiration for this work was equally ignited, over the years, by reflective hikes along the Quinnipiac River's evening banks, long uninterrupted Harbor views provided by I-95 congestion and pacing under the watchful recessed eyes of downtown gargoyles. Here, now, you are invited to join the sojourn and kick the logs of New England's primordial fires. Turn these renewed leaves and rekindle the wondrous history of New Haven. Luckily, it is a history possessed.

## Chapter 1

# The Night of the Wakemanite Ritual

*I have seen a twig of…witch-hazel…which had been gathered on the second
of May (observe this), wound round with some dozens of yards of red thread,
placed visible in the window to act as a charm in keeping witches and Boogle-bees
from the house.*
Gypsy Sorcery and Fortune Telling
*Charles Godfrey Leland, 1891*

*It was the Yuletide, that men call Christmas though they know in their hearts it is
older than Bethlehem and Babylon, older than Memphis and mankind. It was the
Yuletide, and I had come at last to the ancient sea town where my people had dwelt.*
*"The Festival"*
*H.P. Lovecraft, 1923*

*On Christmas Eve in an old house, a strange tale…*
The Turn of the Screw
*Henry James, 1898*

C hristmas Eve is traditionally marked by holly and ivy, eggnog and games,
but strangely enough, in what seems an antithesis to the holy night, holidays
past were celebrated with fireside ghost stories. Charles Dickens's *A Christmas
Carol* immediately comes to mind. This lost tradition of sharing "scary ghost
stories" at Christmastime beckons in a musical footnote each season when Andy
Williams croons, "It's the Most Wonderful Time of the Year." No matter what

Families once gathered around fireplaces on Christmas Eve to hear ghostly tales. From the facial expressions in this illustration, the narrator must be sharing a particularly frightening encounter, perhaps even the events associated with the night of the Wakemanite ritual. *"A Ghost Story," from the* Illustrated London News, *December 24, 1864. Michael J. Bielawa Collection.*

ancient source ushered such a supernatural sentiment into being, lurking evil crossed a New Haven threshold as church bells tolled midnight on December 24, 1855. Inside a forsaken cottage near Munson Street events would molder into Christmas Eve terror tales for many unholy nights to come.

The wooden one-and-a-half-story structure was home to an assortment of New Haven waifs and strays. Old widow Wakeman and her fifty-two-

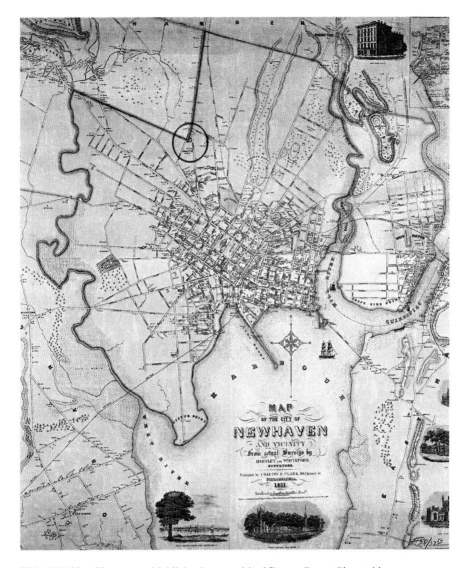

This 1851 New Haven map highlights long-vanished Beaver Street. Situated in a lane between Dixwell and Goffe Streets, Wakemanite cult members journeyed to this neighborhood from as far away as North Branford, Connecticut, during the early 1850s. *Courtesy of the New Haven Museum Photo Archives.*

year-old brother (some said half brother), Samuel Sly, owned the house. Those finding refuge here, including Thankful Stone Hersey and Abigail Sables, formed a special family. Located in the western part of town, the abode was tucked among Beaver Street's byzantine alleys, above Webster

Street and between Dixwell and Goffe Streets. New Haven directories dating from the mid-1850s list Mrs. Rhoda Wakeman's address as being the fourth house south of Munson Street. (The path that Beaver Street once followed corresponds to present-day Orchard Street.) Approaching the ramshackle Wakeman place, the city's antebellum citizens surely crossed to the other side of the lane.

Neighbors shook their heads when considering the wrinkled seventy-year-old crone. The widow dressed, it was noted, in an entirely "veiled" manner. There was something perplexingly familiar about the way she carried herself; someone noted that Mrs. Wakeman resembled the incarnation of a seventeenth-century Salem witch.

Rhoda Sly was born in Huntington, Connecticut, in 1786. She probably wasn't quite fourteen years of age when she married twenty-three-year-old Ira Wakeman of Greenfield Hill, a brutish and abusive man, who, according to the couple's son, was prone to bring a razor to bed and threaten to kill Rhoda should she read the Bible. Around the early 1830s, Mrs. Wakeman had taken to mysticism and dubbed herself "the Prophetess." There was a longstanding rumor, beginning with Ira's death in 1833, that he'd been murdered by his wife. Widow Wakeman eked out a minimal sustenance by weaving, until her strange visions and rants compelled both her and brother,

Revered by Wakemanites as "the Seer," frail and bespectacled old Rhoda Wakeman preached to her New Haven congregation that an anxious demon sought her destruction and that her death would compel the world's demise. *From the Collection of the Sterling and Francine Clark Art Institute Library, Williamstown, Massachusetts.*

Samuel, to flee Fairfield.[1] For a while, Wakeman and Sly provided potions out of one of the jumbled shanties abutting the walls of New Haven's Grove Street Cemetery. Folks visiting that strange Ashmun Street business strayed into a world of poultices, strange restitution syrups and magical elixirs. Over the course of her seventeen years in the City of Elms, the widow solidified her stature as a "seer."

Mrs. Wakeman's surreal sermons expressed how she'd been viciously murdered by her husband, Ira, three decades earlier. Dead for seven hours, the widow enthusiastically recalled how her spirit toured heaven escorted by two sword-wielding angels. Wakeman joyously related meeting Jesus Christ. The old woman's fevered delusions attracted a couple dozen or so converts, lost souls or merely simpleminded farmers, factory workers, shoemakers and husbands and wives. Many of these disciples came from neighboring Hamden and as far away as North Branford, Connecticut, to hear Wakeman's wild prophecies. Locals dubbed these fanatical cult members Wakemanites. Believers, in turn, addressed their savior, Mrs. Wakeman, as the Messenger and adoringly as the Prophetess. One vital doctrine espoused by the Wakemanites' convoluted canon included the deluded belief that the End of Days would erupt should the Prophetess suddenly die.

Enter Justus W. Matthews. The thirty-five-year-old mechanic worked in the Whitneyville Pistol Factory, not far from Mrs. Wakeman's cottage (Justus lived in Hamden with his wife and four children). Once, he'd been a Wakemanite in good standing; Matthews even borrowed $200 from a savings association so he could tithe the Prophetess (the bank's dunning for that loan would commence soon). However, over the past several weeks Matthews's attendance at Wakemanite gatherings had been noticeably lacking. The widow's health simultaneously began to suffer; Mrs. Wakeman complained of being cursed by an evil spirit. This entity, she warned, was very near at hand. The Prophetess pointed a gnarled finger at none other than Justus Matthews. The factory employee was the unwitting receptacle for the demon vexing Mrs. Wakeman. Immediately the Wakemanites were thrust into a quandary. Should Mrs. Wakeman fall dead, their faith decreed, the world would simply cease. Fearful for the well being of the Prophetess and their own lives, as well as the fate of the earth, believers needed to deal with Justus W. Matthews.

The devil inside Matthews had a long and sinister lineage according to the Wakemanites. Initially, the entity resided in Ira Wakeman, Rhoda's husband; then it entered, Eben Gould of Greenfield Hill (Mrs. Wakeman's son-in-

The Wakemanites were not alone. Spiritualism exploded across antebellum America with a fury. This contemporary illustration sensationalizes the devilish behavior of adherents. *From J.W. Daniels's* Spiritualism Versus Christianity; Or, Spiritualism Thoroughly Exposed.

One of the nineteenth century's greatest scientific minds, Yale professor Benjamin Silliman (1779–1864), provided the first chemical analysis of an American meteorite. When the Weston Meteorite exploded through the atmosphere in 1807, the fiery globe may have been witnessed by Rhoda Wakeman, who, at the time, lived in the vicinity. Years later the Prophetess requested that Silliman analyze poison sent to her by a supposed demon. *Courtesy of PictureHistory.com.*

law); from there the evil spirit passed on to Wakemanite Amos Hunt, who, according to the cult, tried to poison the Prophetess in late November 1855. Hunt supposedly baked a cake and liberally peppered it with arsenic to prove beyond doubt that Mrs. Wakeman was truly immortal. Or maybe it was an attempted murder. The poison made the old lady seriously ill but, like Rasputin, she survived (obviously to the Wakemanites) due to her heightened supernatural gifts. The Prophetess had her brother bring the cake to Yale for analysis. Professor Silliman agreed to conduct the experiments but was informed by Sly that Mrs. Wakeman had already identified the malign concoction. The good professor invited her to share this knowledge. The Prophetess sent word back that since routine poisons had no effect on her, Hunt prepared a witch's brew consisting of "the brains of a man, the oil of men's bones, the eyes of dogs, the brains of cats, the hearts of dogs, the eyes of roosters, garden basil, topaz stone, copper, platina, and the entrails of common toads."

Amos Hunt was damned by the Wakemanites while the Prophetess's miraculous recovery empowered her already zealot followers. Dogged, or shaken-down, by "Uncle Sammy" Sly and his sister, Hunt agreed to pay a $500 restitution. Eventually, the demon abandoned Hunt and took over Justus Matthews. One follower, Polly A. Sanford, calmly explained, "After [Matthews] got it, he went home, and his wife [Mehetable] went into convulsions, and seemed to know that her husband had an evil spirit." Mehetable sensed this "unseen power" within Justus. The Hamden wife shivered, "There was something dreadful in [Justus Matthews's] appearance."

In this small New Haven home, Rhoda Wakeman and Samuel Sly concocted strange potions and elixirs to be sold from a stall near the Grove Street Cemetery. Spiritualism, extraordinary sermons, an exorcism and at least one ritual killing all occurred within these walls. *From the Collection of the Sterling and Francine Clark Art Institute Library, Williamstown, Massachusetts.*

No one on earth wanted the world to survive more than Justus W. Matthews. He volunteered to have the evil spirit cast out from his body. The sullen "man of sin" agreed to be at Mrs. Wakeman's cottage. It was already determined how Matthews, and the demon, would be confronted.

Sunday, December 23, 1855, was selected for the ceremony's commencement. The Wakemanite penchant for magic suggests they would not have made this a random date; it's been an overlooked fact that the cult chose to meet Justus Matthews during a full moon. Congregates gathered

To save the world from destruction, Justus Mathews was bound in this very room while the demented Samuel Sly attacked a demon with a magic witch hazel branch. *From the Collection of the Sterling and Francine Clark Art Institute Library, Williamstown, Massachusetts.*

throughout the day and late into the evening, singing and praying for the Prophetess's safety. Earlier in the week, much discussion had been focused on collecting a particular specimen of wood required to successfully beat the devil out of Matthews. Because of its purported magical properties, witch hazel became the mystical weapon of preference. The wood held special powers. When this bark was brewed, according to Wakemanite Thankful S. Hersey, imbibing its tea subdued dark forces. Another of the Wakemanite believers, African American Josiah Jackson, explained that he'd been gifted with a cane of witch hazel to combat evil spirits; and although he swore it was Negroes who were usually credited with such "conjuration powers," Jackson vigorously exhorted, "but I got this idea from *white folks*"—the Wakemanites.

There'd be no difficulty locating a branch. Samuel Sly was adept at cultivating the plant known for its telltale yellow winter-season bloom; he harvested and sold the numinous herb at market. It was agreed that the devil within Matthews was so powerful that a cup of tea may not work. Sly would need to gather a bough, a thick bough, of witch hazel. But maybe just one really hard smack, said Jackson to fellow cult members, would be enough to exercise the demon.

Matthews arrived at the Wakemanite sanctuary off Beaver Street somewhere between ten and eleven o'clock at night on December 23. Ghost-laden Christmas Eve would awaken in a matter of an hour or two.

In the upstairs room, the Prophetess preached and swayed and yowled of illness while her congregants sang and prayed. The devil inside Justus

Tiny Whitneyville—part of the town of Hamden, Connecticut—hosts an enormous industrial history. Eli Whitney trumpeted the concept of mass production and interchangeable parts here and his son, Eli Whitney Jr., continued manufacturing guns in the armory pictured on the right. A willing victim of exorcism and ultimately human sacrifice, Wakemanite Justus Matthews, was a mechanic in the Eli Whitney complex. *Illustration from John Warner Barber's* Connecticut Historical Collections. *Courtesy of the Michael J. Bielawa Collection.*

Matthews would be cast out this night. The possessed man readily agreed to do his part to save Mrs. Wakeman and the world. But first, precautions required careful implementation. A handkerchief and a length of strong cord were produced. The "man of sin" needed blindfolding so his eyes couldn't subconsciously, or by Satan's will, enchant those around him. Black silk would darken Matthew's vision—this cloth's sacred properties, the Wakemanites believed, repelled evil. Justus's hands also needed to be secured behind his back so it'd be impossible for him to conjure spells. The world's rescuers peered at each other in the attic gloom. Who would be brave enough to approach the entity downstairs, slowly tilting back and forth in the old rocking chair? Mrs. Polly Sanborn mumbled something. She agreed to come within reach of the demon-man. The Wakemanites nodded assent. Polly was the one person, they felt, least susceptible to suffer paranormal attack from Justus—she was his sister.

Between the hours of midnight and four o'clock in the morning, Uncle Sammy Sly checked on the welfare of the bound man. During one of Sly's absences,

Yale graduate John Dutton Candee (1819–1888) served on the initial coroner's jury of inquest concerning the death of Justus Matthews. During the subsequent murder trial, Candee and E.K. Foster were named as the state's prosecution team. Following his career in law, attorney Candee turned to his true calling: journalism. Candee worked briefly at the *New Haven Journal and Courier* before becoming longtime editor of the *Bridgeport Standard*. *Courtesy of the Connecticut State Library.*

the Wakemanites' solemn chants were interrupted by disturbing noises in the room below. Loud thrashing could be heard as well as what definitely resembled gurgling. Mr. and Mrs. Sanford ran to the home's lower level only to discover the door secured from within. The Prophetess wasn't the least concerned.

The sun rose wearily on Monday, Christmas Eve Day 1855. It had been just a few hours after the ritual when Wakemanite Almeron Sanford walked back to Hamden and found Justus Matthews's son, Willard. He bid him to go down to New Haven in search of his absent father. The bloody scene the Matthews boy confronted inside Mrs. Wakeman's home sent the young man screaming into the street. Justus lay on his side in the middle of the room, and blood had pooled thickly around his body. Blood and hair were splattered on a cot and the interior door. Shocked policemen dragged the Wakemanites into custody. Slowly the confusing and unbelievable cult members' testimony came into gory focus. Elder Sly had slammed Matthews in the side of the head with a two-foot-long, two-inch-diameter witch hazel wand. Knocked onto the floor, Sly continued hitting the semiconscious man with the club. Justus was gasping for air but never struggled. Sly raised Matthews's head and with a small pocketknife repeatedly slashed and gouged the fettered man's throat. In an attempt to release the demon, Uncle Sammy admitted to stabbing a large fork over and over into the dying man's bosom. Widow Wakeman, Samuel Sly and Thankful Hersey, who'd assisted

Mystic healer Samuel Sly collected magic herbs in and around New Haven. He provided fellow Wakemanite Josiah Jackson with a witch hazel cane to combat evil spirits. Contemporary writers noted Samuel Sly's "eyes of hazel, are small, dreamy and fanatical." *From the Collection of the Sterling and Francine Clark Art Institute Library, Williamstown, Massachusetts.*

Uncle Sammy before the crime by suggesting witch hazel as a weapon and afterward by helping to conceal and destroy evidence, were remanded to jail where they awaited trial. The New Haven *Columbian Register* sarcastically intoned, "It remains to be seen whether the world will be destroyed by keeping this wonderful prophetess [incarcerated]." But the newspaper should have asked another question: By executing Matthews did Samuel Sly release a demon on the world?

Prowling ghosts and evil spirits of Christmas Eve refused to leave the hills around New Haven. Sam Perkins looked out his front window on the snowy world this first day of 1856. The blacksmith lived in one of the dozen or so buildings in Woodbridge center; his home faced the main road on the corner where the shunpike veered off toward Carrington

Hill. Gloomy country up in those woods, especially during winter, Perkins mused. He was startled from his thoughts when a lone horse walked by, dragging sleigh runners. Strange, the burly fellow thought, there being no rider or carriage. After a moment or so, a barking dog jogged along after the gelding. The beast stopped a short distance away at the shed beside Uriah Clinton's public house. Five hours later, and with still no one claiming the animals, Perkins went down to the hotel. The blacksmith recognized these animals as belonging to a neighboring famer, Enoch Sperry. For the last year, Sperry had been struggling with his health; the side of his face had been paralyzed and his vision and hearing severely taxed due to stroke. Agitated, the dog paced to and fro, mournfully yelping, pausing periodically to stare questioningly at the horse. Samuel Perkins looked up in the direction of darkening Carrington Hill and frowned. He was determined to get an answer.

About a mile north along the roadside, next to the frozen brook, Perkins's search came to an abrupt conclusion. Retracing the tracks of the now obviously orphaned dog and horse led to the body of Enoch Sperry. Perkins raised a hand to his mouth. Sperry lay there in the snow, nearly decapitated. The head clung to the body by a narrow strip of ligament. The old farmer's wrinkled hand still clutched a handkerchief.

Earlier that day Enoch Sperry paced the familiar stone steps leading from his farmhouse door and began the two-mile jaunt into town. The Sperry

Nehemiah Day Sperry (1827–1911) was secretary of state of Connecticut when a deranged Wakemanite attacked and killed his father, Enoch, near their Woodbridge home. Sperry's powerful position in the state may have had a bearing on the subsequent murder trial. Nehemiah served as a Connecticut congressman from 1895 to 1911. *Courtesy Connecticut State Library.*

estate was a well-known landmark, in both Woodbridge and across the state. One of Enoch's sons, Nehemiah Day Sperry, was an influential member of the early Republican Party and was presently serving as Connecticut's secretary of state. Four decades later, at the turn of the twentieth century, he'd be elected to Congress. N.D. Sperry's lofty position in New Haven County would not bode well for his father's murderer.

Enoch decided that New Year's Day was the perfect time to retrieve the carriage for his sleigh, known as a sled box. He'd walked with his dog and horse, dragging the runners, only a short distance from the scent of his home's chimney when Charles Sanford suddenly appeared out of the dense woods. The night before, on New Year's Eve, just one week following the Justus Matthews exorcism and killing, Charles went berserk at a Methodist church meeting in Bethany. Stamping about the altar, he demanded that the minister leave the church. Then, Sanford stalked the desolate hills of Woodbridge cradling an ax and three-foot-long hazel club, which he'd sharpened into a stake at both ends. Words resembling the wild and Wakemanite-familiar incantations of the Prophetess were scratched into to the stick. He'd attended the fanatics' meetings, most certainly because of his relationship to the group's members. He was the nephew of Mr. and Mrs. Almeron Sanford and nephew to Julia Davis. In fact, Charles was related, through marriage, to the murdered Justus Matthews. There was speculation that the Christmas Eve ritual killing had snapped Sanford's already eggshell-fragile mind, prompting him to wander the Woodbridge countryside in search of victims to sacrifice.

The old farmer had always befriended Charles, whom the

The Wakemanites were defended at their trial by powerful officials. One of their attorneys was Henry Dutton (1796–1869) the Kent Professor of Law at Yale. A year prior to representing the Wakemanites, Dutton had lost his reelection bid for governor. *Courtesy Connecticut State Library.*

community recognized as mentally ill. In fact, Enoch knew the Sanford family, including Wakemanites Almeron and Polly. (There was also another surprising connection to Mr. Sperry and the Wakemanites; seeking relief from his own maladies, Enoch had consulted Rhoda Wakeman in her shop, requesting whatever medicinal herbs she might divine as necessary.) On that lonely snow-covered road, Enoch and Sanford may have exchanged pleasantries at first, for the gash over Sperry's right eye proved that they had initially faced one another. Once Sperry was on the ground, however, young Charles raised his ax again and again trying to sever the poor man's head.

Wiping the blood from the pocked metal with snow, Charles rambled off into the hills. He next found Philip Samson, a towering African American woodsman collecting timber. His first inclination was to kill the sawyer, but Charles thought better of confronting a large man; so he continued his march into the brush. A short distance away, the incoherent Sanford stumbled on the home of Ichabod Umberfield. The servant, Lucy Deming, was in the front room holding her baby when the madman burst in. Farmer Ichabod, out back chopping wood, heard the ruckus and lumbered into the house through the kitchen. The servant had hidden in a bedroom with her child. Umberfield bid the disheveled young fellow be comfortable and sit with him beside the fire. "Take your time," Ichabod calmly spoke, "But tell me, what ails you son. Can I help?" They were the kindhearted man's last words. Charles Sanford sprung from his chair and brought the ax down on his second victim. The murderer ran from the house while Deming bolted the doors behind him. That was when the posse arrived.

Composed mostly of rural laborers, the group had taken to the woods armed with clubs and pitchforks. Willis Doolittle and Enos Gorham were the first to run down the culprit. Charles Sanford was coming out of the forest and heading back toward the Umberfield farmhouse. The Wakemanite stated that he was going there to "kill the rest of them." The vigilantes didn't have time to digest Sanford's comment. The twenty-eight-year-old charged into the group of eight men swinging his ax. Doolittle barely missed being killed when the blunt bottom of Sanford's ax head came crashing down on his shoulder. Lewis Peck raised a pitchfork and pressed the tines against the demented man's heaving chest. The distraction allowed Gorham to sneak around the madman and bash him over the head with a club.

In mid-January 1856, a grand jury indicted Samuel Sly as principal, and his sister and Thankful Hersey as accessories, to the murder of Justus Matthews. The Prophetess "wept like an infant," reported the *Hartford Daily Courant*. Thankful Hersey pointed at the cult leader and said, "They little know what they are about in shutting up that person here [in jail]." The Wakemanite clan went on trial that spring. They were defended by former governor Henry Dutton (the last Connecticut Whig to hold the position) and Joseph Sheldon Jr. The prosecution was handled by District Attorney Eleazer Kingsbury Foster and John D. Candee. The presiding judges were Joel Hinman and Loren Pinckney Waldo. The defendants pleaded not guilty. The trial didn't last long, and the verdict was expected. Widow Wakeman, Samuel Sly and Thankful S. Hersey were found not guilty due to reason of insanity. In a separate trial, Charles Sanford was found guilty of murder and condemned to hang. Sanford avoided the noose but came to a dreadful end when he suddenly fell ill in prison and succumbed to smallpox.

"Ichabod Umberfield...who was murdered by a maniac." Kindhearted farmer Ichabod Umberfield was decapitated by Charles Sanford; he is buried in the Sperry Cemetery, Bethany, Connecticut. Umberfield's gravestone forever whispers of the Wakemanite madness. *Photograph by Michael J. Bielawa.*

## THE AFTERMATH OF THE WAKEMANITES

**Josiah Jackson** was correct when he said that his witch hazel walking stick would keep him from harm. He never went to trial. Taken into custody during the Justus Matthews investigation, he was released into the care of James F. Babcock, Connecticut state senator and editor of the *New Haven Palladium*. Babcock, a political powerhouse, was a confidant to Abraham Lincoln. During his 1860 campaign swing through Connecticut, the future president stayed at Babcock's Fair Haven mansion. The possibility exists that Lincoln, himself fascinated with spiritualism, may have met Jackson.

**Amos Hunt,** who'd been accused of trying to poison the Prophetess, continued his forays into the supernatural. The former Wakemanite became a clock maker. Then, sometime during the 1870s, he added the title of "Doctor" to his name and anointed himself a "clairvoyant physician." His trances created national news when the father of murder victim Mary Stannard consulted him. Hunt's visions accurately described specifics about the murder site and weapon, which up to that point hadn't been known. Seemingly unable to shake a lifetime of run-ins with mysterious killings and the law, in 1886, a sheet of his memorandum paper turned up in a drowned man's pockets. The top of the paper was imprinted: "A. Hunt, corner of Jackson and Clay Streets."

Hunt disavowed any knowledge of the man, whose death was later ruled a suicide. Three years later, New Haven health officials cited Hunt when the "doctor" failed to report contagious diseases contributing to the death of his patients.

**Samuel "Uncle Sammy" Sly** never abandoned his passionate Wakemanite beliefs. Deemed criminally insane, he'd find himself behind bars for the rest of his life. Years of praying on the prison's stone floors disfigured and bloated Sly's knees. For a decade following the Wakemanite trial, Uncle Sammy was a model prisoner. However, just as the Civil War ended, he became consumed by the belief that he was the embodiment of the Prophet Elijah and commenced a hunger strike. He died in the New Haven County Jail and Workhouse on June 30, 1865.

**Thankful Stone Hersey,** like the Prophetess, was charged in the superior court of New Haven County with being accessory to murder. Acquitted because of insanity, the fifty-six-year-old Hersey was placed in New Haven Jail. The cultured woman generated no threat to society but was determined incapable of looking after her own welfare. A wealthy retired sea captain, Samuel E. Foote, paid the "requisite bonds for the protection of the community against her" and invited Hersey into his Whitney Avenue home. The house and palatial grounds, where Captain Foote conducted horticulture and agriculture experiments, were known as Windy Knowe. Foote often hosted open-minded salons during his eight-year stay in New Haven; abolitionist Wendell Phillips and radical proslavery advocate George Fitzhugh debated under his roof. Hersey lived quite peacefully, showing no signs of instability, often sewing for her adopted family. Twenty-five months after her trial, Thankful Hersey died on May 12, 1857. Informed of her passing, Samuel Sly commented, "It is different from what was expected."

**Rhoda Wakeman** lived the remainder of her days incarcerated. She died (once again, and forever) in the year 1859.

Throughout her remaining days, Rhoda Wakeman continued to delve into scripture, undoubtedly twisting verses into her own bizarre apocalyptic worldview. *From the Collection of the Sterling and Francine Clark Art Institute Library, Williamstown, Massachusetts.*

**Willard Matthews,** whose father, Justus, was the focus of the Wakemanites' fury, proved resilient. A little over three years after the tragedy, he married Sarah M. Merwin of Woodbridge. Together they remained in Hamden, Connecticut, working the family farm in the town's West Woods District. Willard Matthews lived into the twentieth century.

## Chapter 2

# The Haunted Lightship of
# New Haven Harbor

*"About this time of year," he said, studying the murk and fog, "something comes
to visit the lighthouse."*
*"The Fog Horn"*
*Ray Bradbury, 1951*

*It was something ghostly, horrible beyond words, and it moved in my grip. It was
like the body of a man long drowned, and yet it moved...*
*"The Upper Berth"*
*F. Marion Crawford, 1894*

S ome voyages may not seem far, but the destination is otherworldly.
Just a short journey up the coast from New Haven, along a well-worn
cobblestone lane, inside one of Mystic Seaport's nautical buildings, hangs an
old ship's quarterpanel. It is all that remains of the *Robert P. King*, a forgotten
lightship once anchored at the mouth of New Haven Harbor. The gold
letters of the narrow six-foot board still beckons to those willing to listen. Its
ornately carved eagle design whispers of mutiny and murder and the *Robert
P. King's* dreaded shrieking ghost.

The nefarious narrative of New Haven's many lightships is little recalled.
Perhaps their histories' erasure is the result of a willful abandonment due
to the strange, wild and inexplicable events that took place on their decks.
Listen now to the salvaged chronicle of one of New England's greatest
supernatural maritime stories.

Throughout the first three-quarters of the nineteenth century, those sailors plying the hectic waterway of Long Island Sound looked distrustfully on New Haven Harbor. Seeking safety in times of treacherous weather, ships needed to sail far north into this wide port in order to escape the waves and wind. To remedy this dire situation, the government undertook the building of a series of stone breakwaters. The huge engineering task began in 1880, when a three-thousand-foot-long wall was assembled on the east side of the harbor's mouth. A decade later, another breakwater was being built about three hundred feet longer and averaging thirty-eight feet in height. It extended from Ludington Rock westward. However, a majority of old salts saw the newest breakwater, with its inadequate lighting and savage currents, as creating a host of potential disasters.

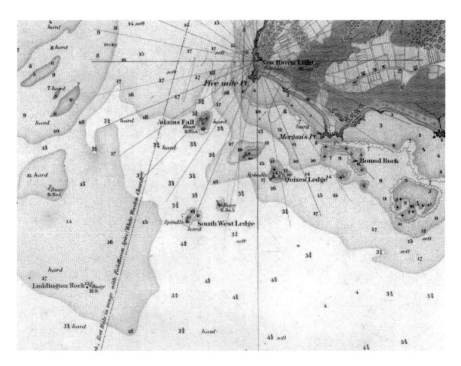

Numerous rocks and obstructions are readily visible on this 1846 nautical chart. One particular hazard to navigation was Southwest Ledge, seen here at the harbor's entrance (in the lower middle of this map). New Haven Light at Five Mile Point proved insufficient to deal with these dangers. *From* New Haven Harbor… Survey of the Coast.

To protect its fleet, as well as serve the public good, the New Haven Steamboat Company took matters into its own coal-calloused hands. As the early spring sun of 1893 tossed pearls into the spray and swells of New Haven Harbor, the former New London fishing smack, *Martha Emma*, sailed down from Belle Dock to take its position at the harbor's mouth as a lightship. Stationed about a mile and a half southwest of the new breakwater, the vessel had been refitted with a cabin for the two men maintaining the ship. The *Martha Emma* was painted black, but brightly rendered across both its sides were the words "New Haven Steamship Company Lightship." At night, and during inclement weather, two illuminated eight-inch globes were hung from the masts.

Nature, or perhaps the unnatural, had charted a course for the harbor's lightships. Within weeks of its initial positioning, the *Martha Emma* was struck by lightning and cast adrift. Tragedy struck again a few months later during October 1893, when a strong gale cut its cable and sent the ship rolling uncontrollably into stormy seas. The light keeper, Captain George Johnson, and his assistant, Fred Hansen, attempted to make Stratford Light but quickly realized their only salvation was lashing themselves to the mast. Smashing onto a rocky ledge, the *Martha Emma* was pounded for godless hours by towering waves. With the boat taking on water and in danger of sinking, the men finally retreated high into the rigging. As the storm abated and the battered light keepers strained to witness the miracle of dawn, they swam two hundred yards for Merwin's Point, located in the Woodmont section of Milford, Connecticut.

The next day, on foot and in carriages, one thousand people ventured to Woodmont's shore to glimpse the wreck. Its tattered sails, fog bell and furniture were salvaged by the steamship company; what remained was carted away by Milford's would-be Mooncussers, the local relic hunters. The schooner's wooden skeleton lingered just over a year, until a December 1894 storm splintered the barnacled remnants, and the *Martha Emma* was no more.

The next lightship to service New Haven Harbor was the *Crystal Wave*, a sloop once part of Fair Haven's oystering fleet. Captain W.H. Shutter was named the new keeper. Within three weeks, the breakwater's strong tidal currents proved that a steady anchorage was untenable for the craft. The harbor again sank into darkness.

In the autumn of 1894, Parker Jones Hall, owner of the schooner *Robert P. King*, was contracted to maintain the latest lightship. Hall was regarded as one of New England's most accomplished and courageous coastermen. As if ordained by fate, Parker had been born into a sea-rescuing family on June 16, 1862, in the South Shore town of Marshfield, Massachusetts. When the boy turned twelve

Word on the New Haven docks circulated that Captain Hall's schooner, the *Robert P. King*, was haunted. Well known in the coaster business for both his short temper as well as his severe stutter, the captain himself may have invited the strange happenings onboard. According to Parker's friend John F. Leavitt, Hall "violated every ancient superstition of the seafaring profession. Blue paint he used in profusion, hatch covers flipped over on their backs, and he whistled [and] stuck knives in masts." Hall is pictured here in 1943, fifty-one years after the attempted mutiny and bizarre events plagued the *King. Copyright Mystic Seaport, Mystic, Connecticut, #1982.120.51.39.*

years of age, his father, George, was appointed the first keeper of the Gurnett Island Life-Saving Station, located at the mouth of Plymouth Bay. For twenty years prior, the elder Hall had patrolled the area's beaches as a surfman. A year later, in 1875, young Parker ran off to sea at the age of thirteen. He captained a yacht in Boston Harbor for a few seasons before turning to the coastal trade, transporting fish, lumber and cement.

Hall originally took possession of the *Robert P. King* at a government auction in Woods Hole, Massachusetts, during 1890. The two-master had been confiscated and branded a pirate. This ship was already shrouded in a mysterious and tragic past. Weighing 113 tons, it had been constructed in Philadelphia, according to maritime historian Charles F. Sayle, back in 1847, as a herm brig. Sadly, the craft was built to provide a Middle Passage hell as a slaver running between Africa and Cuba. Later it was refitted for whaling expeditions. As if to make amends for its early blood voyages, it served during the Civil War in the naval blockade of the South, as a mortar station on the James River. By the time Captain Hall claimed it, the ship had been registered as a schooner and seen many names: the *Centurion*, the *Melville*, the *King* and an assortment of ever-shifting monikers, all used to solicit valuable cargos only to have the crew fence their goods to the highest bidder.

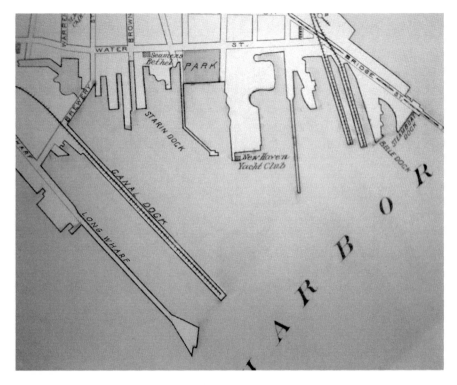

During the nineteenth century, an assortment of New Haven docks with their related warehouses, saloons and businesses, both legal and illicit, saw tall ships arrive from around the globe. Long Wharf at one point extended 3,480 feet into the harbor. Familiar territory for Captain Parker Hall, this map dates from the period when he operated the harbor's lightship. The schooner *Robert P. King* and other vessels put into Belle Dock for repairs. *Courtesy of the Connecticut State Library.*

By 1894, it was deemed prudent by the New Haven Steamship Company to provide a lightship on a strictly seasonal basis, the six months from autumn to spring. Captain Hall looked forward to continuing the family tradition as a lifesaver. The thirty-two-year-old seaman oversaw the installation of a resounding fog bell as well as the dual lights that were raised nightly. The refitted *Robert P. King* hoisted sail, departing Belle Dock for the brief journey to the harbor's mouth. It would proudly serve New Haven and Long Island Sound in its role as a lightship.

It was merely a matter of tides before the schooner's ghostly reality began to wander New Haven's dockside. During Captain Hall's time at the schooner's wheel, he scoffed when crews complained about disembodied voices plaguing their coastal trips. It wasn't until the winter of 1895–96 that the skipper began experiencing strange events firsthand off the shore of New Haven. Hall could not assemble a crew; no sailor could be enticed to remain aboard. It became obvious something inhabited the *Robert P. King*. In a May 5, 1896 New Haven *Evening Register* interview, the captain explained, "Yes sir, there has been a ghost on board my vessel while I have been located off the breakwater." This entity raucously manifested itself. Skipper Hall recounted, "I first had occasion to notice this mystery one day while sitting at the table. I heard some person call out my name. The noise seemed to come from the deck, and I immediately went up there and looked around. There was no one to be found. I had a sailor with me in the cabin at the time, and he also heard the call plainly." Initially the captain reasoned someone must be perpetrating an elaborate joke. Despite searching the ship stem to stern, no source was ever located. After the first incident, the voice shouted both day and night; it demanded Hall by name and also cried out for help. During the quiet moments of deep night, hysterical laugher emanated from the rigging, but it was the unearthly shrieks that chased frightened crews back to shore. Captain Hall was not a drinking man, and he was considered quite credible; New Haven longshoremen and those associated with the city's harbor businesses believed the tales. When questioned about a possible supernatural cause of the voice, Hall postulated, "I think that the vessel probably left a dying man out at sea sometime. The man was not saved when he could have been by the crew of this vessel, and I think that it is this man's ghost we have been hearing." When the six-month, wintertime lightship duty ended and Hall began his traditional summertime coastal route, sailors continued to shun the haunted ship. The shrieks stalked Hall, summoning him at least once a week. After several seasons the captain eventually came to grips with the bizarre entity. Parker Hall would go on record as saying that he'd learned to coexist with the voice.

But Parker Hall was not completely forthcoming about every possible source for this terrifying shriek, and it was strange that he would forget. The *Robert P. King*'s decks were swathed in blood just a handful of weeks before embarking on its initial lightship duty off New Haven. The *King*'s tale is an old and familiar one to the waves—of mutiny and mayhem and gore.

It was late June 1894 when skipper Hall departed Augusta with a cargo of Maine lumber bound for New Haven. His crew was all experienced seafaring men, the captain having handpicked them a year earlier on Decoration Day 1893, when the *King* dropped anchor in New Bedford. Hands included John Lobs and two Portuguese brothers from Cape Verde, Charles and Frank Duard. The galley was maintained by Jennie

Built in 1847 as a slave ship, the *Robert P. King* later saw service as a whaler and then worked in the coastal trade. It sailed under many names and aliases. Its most famous skipper, Parker J. Hall, purchased the ship at a government auction after it was confiscated for illegal smuggling. Crewmen frightened by its ghost were known to abandon the *King* while it lay at anchor in New Haven Harbor. *Copyright Mystic Seaport, Mystic, Connecticut, #1976.1.171.12.*

Hardenburgh, Hall's sweetheart. With the cargo unloaded in New Haven, Hall paid Lobs, who went on his way, but the Duard brothers, who were owed $150 each, continued working on the *King*. The next job was to transport Hudson River cement out of Eddyville, New York. But all wasn't well on the schooner. The two sailors had been grumbling for weeks and shirking their duties, even forcing Hall to climb into the rigging with a broken rib he'd sustained a few weeks prior when a pile of lumber fell on him.

Before sailing north, Captain Hall needed to attend to some business in New York City. It was early Sunday, July 22, 1894, when the *Robert P. King* dropped anchor in Flushing Bay between Ricker's Island and College Point, New York. The following day, after breakfast, Hall escorted Miss Hardenburgh into the city, where she remained. His meetings completed, the skipper returned by ferry to College Point, collected his dory at the docks of Max Zehden's Hotel and rowed out to the *King* in a misty rain. It was around nine o'clock at night.

The captain climbed aboard his schooner and called out for assistance. As the Duard brothers and Hall finished securing the dory onto the ship's port side behind the main mast toward the cabin, one of the siblings suddenly smashed the captain across the face with a piece of lumber. Maybe it was a belaying pin; the stunned captain could not have known. Staggering backward, Hall's blurred eyes filled with hot blood; he fell onto the cabin roof landing on his side. In one sweeping gesture, the skipper pulled a revolver and began blindly firing. There was a scream when a bullet found its mark. Frank Duard had been hit in the side below his left arm, the bullet passing through his lung. The captain continued pulling the trigger, and rounds and sparks flew until the other brother, Charles, was grazed on the back of the head. The only thing saving Charles was that he'd turned to witness Frank collapsing.

Then the true horror began aboard the rain-soaked *Robert P. King*. Hall was pummeled by Charles Duard; they wrestled, kicked and gnawed in a life-and-death grip, falling with a thud from the quarterdeck down onto the main deck. The muted sound of Frank dragging his deadweight could be heard in the pelting rain as he slithered across the gore-slick deck. Concealing himself behind a barrel, then the mast and then some canvas, the wounded man pleaded over and over for his brother to "kill, kill, kill" Captain Hall.

The hissing struggle lasted an interminable two hours. Charles Duard had chomped down into Hall's chest and then locked his teeth onto the sightless captain's thumb. Bone crunched as Hall yowled. Charles begged for Frank to help, but the sailor, blood pulsating out from his side, was now motionless. Parker Hall and Charles throttled each other, their hands in a death clasp around each others' throats. Arms and legs entwined in a slow-motion waltz of torture, they rolled across each deck thrashing closer and closer to the railings, but neither dared throw his opponent overboard for fear he too would be dragged into the bay.

Exhausted, the human knot eventually skid into a pool of Frank Duard's blood. Charles demanded his wounded brother grab a capstan bar and finish Hall for good. Frank moaned that he was too far gone. The fight stalled for a moment, and a truce was called as both Charles and Captain Hall checked on the wounded man. Hall went below deck into his cabin, ignoring another pistol he stowed there, and fetched some oakum to stop Frank's bleeding. A doctor was needed, and fast, so the two men made preparations for lowering the dory. As the boat jerked down the lines, both refused to go first, fearing being attacked; so Hall finally stepped in, only to upset the small boat, nearly filling it with water. Stumbling back on deck, he fainted with pain. Charles Duard lunged on the captain, shocking the man into groggy consciousness. Stalemated in a tangle of limbs once more, the two rivals agreed to a second truce and lowered the yawl. They rowed for the nearby schooner, *Hazel Dell*.

Hall was brought aboard the *Dell* while Charles Duard rowed for shore and the police. Covered head to boot in blood, his face horribly swollen, Hall was barely recognizable, let alone capable of speech when he entered his friend Captain Cozzen's cabin.

When the College Point officers arrived, they found half a dozen or so sailors with Hall, standing in the rain aboard the *King*. The ship's lanterns swayed dim beams down on the barely conscience body of Frank Duard, his clothes saturated with blood. The sailor raised a weak and oozing arm. He pointed at Hall. The captain was instantly arrested and hauled away in handcuffs to College Point jail. Parker Hall telegraphed a brief message to his father in Duxbury, Massachusetts:

*Mutiny on the* King, *I am in jail. Men dying in hospital.*

Six days later, Frank Duard died in Flushing Hospital. Captain Hall's murder trial began October 16, 1894.

The dying testimony Frank Duard provided in the hospital was allowed admissible. Charles Duard took the witness stand corroborating his brother Frank's last words: Captain Parker Hall attacked them without provocation. They figured Hall had it in mind to kill them so he wouldn't have to pay their salaries.

Both prosecution and defense lawyers detailed the extensive fight while the skipper testified that he shot in self-defense. He explained that it was the Duard brothers who had instigated the violence in order to seize the ship and steal the cash they'd anticipated Hall had received during his visit to the city.

The trial lasted two days. In just over half an hour, the jury acquitted Captain Hall. While the judge's gavel fruitlessly demanded order, the skipper's two sisters, brother, aged parents and many Massachusetts friends swelled around the joyous Yankee. A telegraph message was soon received back in Duxbury, setting off a cacophony of church and fire bells, wild fireworks and glorious bonfires.

Within seventy-two hours of his not guilty verdict, newspapers announced that the *Robert P. King*, with Parker Hall acting as keeper, would become the latest lightship to operate off the New Haven breakwater. The schooner would go on to save a number of seamen, some of whom even leapt to safety onto the lightship's decks when their own vessel rolled by out of control.

During a particularly vicious late January 1897 storm, the icy winds and waves scuttled the *Angler*, a schooner on its way from Perth Amboy, New Jersey, to New London with a load of coal. Grounded on the west side of New Haven Harbor, its stern had been crushed by huge ice floes. On February 3, its port side bulged while ice gashed large holes in the hull. The cargo was being flushed out to sea. Judged unsalvageable, plans were made to remove all working parts and transfer what coal might still be left. Only the hull and barren masts remained intact. Miraculously, Captain Hall singlehandedly restored the craft within twelve months. This would become his favorite schooner. New Haven tars wondered aloud whether the shrieking voice would follow Hall onto his new vessel.

In 1898, when New Haven citizens feared an attack during the Spanish-American War, the federal government placed huge Rodman cannons on the breakwater and put Captain Hall, who still served as the *King*'s light keeper, in charge of the batteries. The *Robert P. King* also housed naval crews maintaining the harbor's submarine mines.

Parker Hall sold the *Robert P. King* the following spring, in 1899, to a West Indies trading company. The old schooner would traverse tropical islands gathering coconuts and logwood before transferring these resources to larger ships heading north. The skipper reflected back on the *King*'s long history and wondered what stories its figurehead might share. Sentiment aside, he became serious as a coffin when stating, "It's well that it cannot, for the stories would hang many men." That same year, plans were made to install a permanent beacon in New Haven Harbor. Named after Congressman Nehemiah D. Sperry, who secured appropriation for the station, Sperry Light was built on the outer breakwater. The lighthouse became operational New Year's Day 1900. Its tower stood in place for a third of a century before finally being razed.

Captain Hall never sailed with a crew again. From Maine down through every port along Long Island Sound, all the way to New York City, he piloted the ninety-two-ton *Angler* alone. He would acquire other ships and continue

*Opposite*: Built in 1899 with funding secured by Congressman Nehemiah Day Sperry, this beacon supplanted the need for a harbor lightship. It was torn down in 1933. *Courtesy of the Michael J. Bielawa Collection.*

to sail, always unaccompanied, for nearly fifty years more. Hall was a fixture in Vineyard Sound and the Nantucket Shoals. In time, Parker Hall was dubbed the Lone Skipper and the King of the Lone Navigators.

During the summer of 1948, the ornery old salt ordered his own gravestone and wrote his epitaph. He died a few days later and was buried in Duxbury. Decorated with an etching of the *Angler*, the New Haven wreck Hall saved, the marker reads:

> *Parker Jones Hall*
> *Master Mariner*
> *June 16, 1862*
> *August 25, 1948*
> *Owner & Master*
> *Of 16 Other Schooners*

The *Robert P. King's* quarterpanel now rests in Mystic Seaport's Shipcarver's Shop. You'll find the building on the museum map. Go there to walk along the cobblestone lanes, hear the sailors' chanteys and see the romantic towering ships' masts. Look out on scenic Mystic River and think on olden whaling days. But know this: when you stand before the *Robert P. King's* name

If only this quarterpanel could speak, what wild sea stories it would tell. Smuggling, mutiny, death and ghosts all bloodied the decks of the schooner *Robert P. King*. This beautiful piece of maritime art can be found at Mystic Seaport. *Courtesy of Mystic Seaport, Mystic, CT. Photograph by Michael J. Bielawa.*

plank, staring down at you in gold and blue, you might just hear a wraith's moan. Is this the voice of a long-dead slave, an overboard sailor left to drown or a mutinous crew member? It is up to you to decipher the whispers.

Just before you turn and leave this weathered building to take your place in the New England sun, be sure to tell Captain Parker Hall, leaning there next to the ancient figurines on the windowsill, about the ghostly voice you just heard.

## Chapter 3

# The Damned Dorm

## Something Wicked Lurks Within Yale

*I have made it a rule to investigate every strange appearance I see, and find out if there is anything wonderful in it.*
*Reverend Timothy Dwight*
*Eighth president of Yale, 1752–1817*

Yale president Timothy Dwight was not disconcerted in the least by the supernatural conundrum he'd been presented by inquisitive, albeit waggish, senior classmen. On March 23, 1814, in response to a question about the possible existence of ghosts, the celebrated theologian grinned; on this subject, the New Haven educator was most definitely well informed. Rubbing his chin in expressive reflection, President Dwight leaned toward the packed room (his vision was quite poor) and confidently replied, "It is within the power of God to make specters appear: there is no contradiction involved in it."[2] Who in that audience could have realized during this early spring lecture that the supreme voice of Yale was presciently gazing thirty years into the future and discussing circumstances that would tragically involve the ghost of his yet unborn grandson.

Ghosts and Yale have long cultivated a gothic association.[3] Yale blue and wisps of beckoning gray have been entwined for two hundred years. Indeed, the school's most persistent spirit took up residence in Berkley College, better known as North Middle dorm, sometime just before the Civil War. Students were exceedingly reticent about detailing paranormal manifestations they'd experienced here. However, word of one North Middle encounter did manage

*Left*: Yale president Timothy Dwight (1752–1817) never balked when presented the question, "Do specters appear?" during a senior class lecture. His response is part of Yale's gothic association with the supernatural. *Image copyright Yale University Art Gallery. Gift of the Class of 1817.*

*Below*: In addition to North Middle, this Elm Street house, built by John Pierpont, a grandson of one of Yale's founders, is supposedly haunted. The home was used as a field hospital by the British when they invaded New Haven in 1779. Bloodstained floors, a wandering ghost and shrunken heads are all part of its history. See note three for more information. *Photograph by Michael J. Bielawa.*

to escape the nineteenth century. A "strange light" was cryptically detailed in the February 13, 1867 issue of the *Yale Courant*. The column explained that this glow "does not seem to be the blaze of an ordinary lamp" and was seen wavering in one of North Middle's padlocked, "uninhabitable, desolate" garret apartments. The newspaper vainly queried classmen and faculty alike looking for an adequate answer to the "phenomenon." Later, an essay, "Is North Middle Haunted?" appeared in the *Yale Literary Magazine* during October 1870. This piece took a tongue-in-cheek view concerning the specter, although editors vigilantly incorporated a serious introduction to the story, noting, "Many are the weird tales that are told of nocturnal visions and phantom visitors" inside the murky recesses of North Middle. During the closing years of the Mauve Decade one student's reminiscence, the *Ways of Yale in the Consulship of Plancus* (1895), recalled the true hope of discovering the dorm's nocturnal phantom. Reporting on an archaeological dig that took place on the former site of North Middle nearly a century after the *Ways of Yale* was published, the *Bulletin of the Archaeological Society of Connecticut* tantalizingly commented that the dorm was haunted. Aside from the cordon of silence surrounding paranormal encounters in this building, additionally lost over the course of countless semesters is the causality of these unspoken supernatural events. Here now is a peek into the lurking darkness residing behind the creaking doors of North Middle's long vanished ruins.

Over the decades as these dorms, lecture halls and chapels were constructed, they were popularly dubbed with regard to their location on campus. Berkley Hall, known as North Middle, is situated fifth from the left. *Courtesy of the Connecticut State Library.*

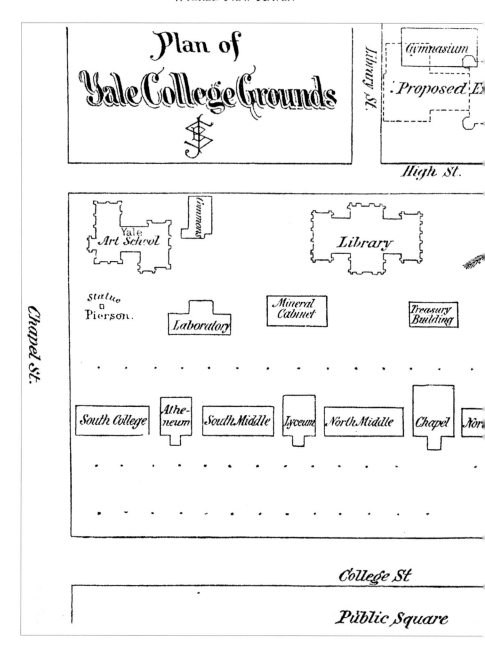

Yale's "Old Brick Row" was constructed between 1750 and 1820. The symmetrical Georgian buildings became identified by a variety of witty monikers: "the shells," "brick barracks" and, perhaps most fittingly during the nation's Industrial Revolution, "the factories." One of the favorite

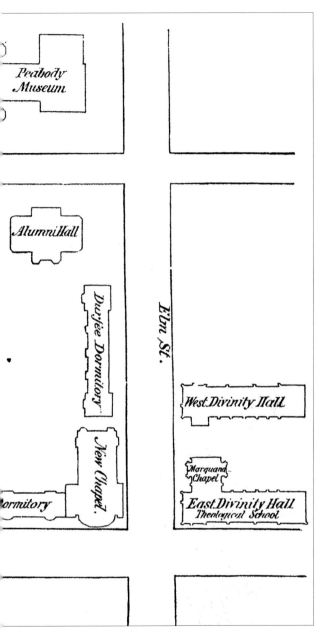

This map identifies the various college structures as they looked during the American Centennial. The Treasury Building, formerly the Trumbull Gallery (behind the Old Chapel), was the site where the banned hazing tradition of "smoking the fresh" resulted in death. *From "Yale College,"* Scribner's Monthly, *April 1876.*

sentinels in this red row was North Middle College. The four-story structure was built between 1801 and 1803 and occupied in 1804. The slate-roofed dorm was razed ninety years later. Connecticut Hall, North Middle's much older twin brother of different architects, provides a present-day bearing for those seeking to pace the straight line delineating the former site of "the factories." North Middle's numerous panes, abutting its street-facing façade, stared out on the ancient gravestones jammed helter-skelter across New Haven's Green. In an attempt to hide the eyesore of crumbling death-heads, a fence was constructed encapsulating the burial ground; but for the first two decades of North Middle's existence, students residing in the dorm's upper floors could not escape the feast of skulls peeking from the sunken earth.

During the summer of 1821, the solemn process of relocating these moldering gravestones to the new Grove Street Cemetery began. It is a fact that no disinterred bodies accompanied these memorials; thus a subterranean population of several thousand deceased New Havenites still resides within the Green's loam. There had circulated a long-standing rictus rumor that the oldest gravestones were brazenly plucked, like forbidden stone fruit, for use as fireplace backs and hearthstones in Yale's dorms. These pilfered tablets had other, even more macabre uses. Locals understood there was something less than savory about the enticing scents emanating from a particular downtown bake house. Henry Blake noted in his 1898 history, *Chronicles of New Haven Green from 1638 to 1862*, how the bone yard's absconded tombstones made for excellent oven floors. The bewitching aroma of oven warm "bread of a certain baker was always known by the trademark cherub's head, or fragment of an epitaph, on the bottom of [his] loaves."

Parapsychologists today might point to the proximity of Yale and the Green's colonial cemetery as a source for unsettled spirits wandering university grounds. Or those stolen gravestones employed in dorm rooms may have enticed a wraith to angrily demand its memorial's return. However, as every reader of *Hamlet* knows, murder most foul classically gives voice to the restless departed, and North Middle saw its share of suspicious slayings.

The strongest case for explaining the haunting of North Middle may have its origins in a crime directly connected to those bleak walls. For years, incoming classmen tolerated the outlawed hazing ritual known as "Smoking the Fresh." As was customary, just as the new school year commenced, Saturday, September 30, 1843, was set aside by upper classmen to brutalize the new blood. Disguising their appearances with wardrobes of terror, juniors blackened their faces and armed themselves (for frightful show) with bludgeons, dirks and knives. Tutors this evening had already resolved outbursts associated with this banned activity. In fact, a new tutor, John Breed Dwight, and his colleague Daniel Rumsey disbursed more than a dozen rowdies who'd rambunctiously gathered in the campus yard. Dwight was twenty-one years of age, having graduated from Yale's law school in

North Middle College. This four-story dormitory could accommodate nearly one hundred students. Popular with seniors up until 1820, the upper floor windows gazed on the ancient boneyard located on the Green. *From W.E. Decrow, Yale and "The City of Elms."*

1840. The noble fellow came from grand New Haven stock; his grandfather, Timothy Dwight, had served as Yale's eighth president. Certainly the Dwight family entertained the possibility that young John might ascend the same academic pinnacle.

Conflicting reports muddle ensuing events of that autumn night, but pieced together, testimony illustrates that at about 9:30 that evening, tutors Dwight and Rumsey responded a second time to the sound of breaking glass and the odor of smoke. Another gang spontaneously passed from the library toward North Middle, shattering windows before racing through campus. Another report has it that the tutors-turned-constables entered one of North Middle's rooms, apartment eighty-four, prompting the hazing students to escape through the windows. All reports state that there was the sound of breaking glass followed by a crowd running. In the dark, Dwight saw one fellow dash for the street; he pursued and, snatching a piece of the garment that was part of the boy's disguise, thrust himself on the student's shoulders and tackled the prankster to the ground. For a moment, they both lay prone in the center of the Old Campus at the southwest corner of the Trumbull Gallery, a fireproof building designed by John Trumbull to exhibit the architect's much more famous paintings.

Dwight had no idea that he was grappling with sophomore Louis Fassitt. The student haled from Philadelphia, where his father, James, was a wealthy merchant. Newspapers confidently reported Fassitt being fifteen years old, but in reality, he had just turned seventeen. The tutor pinned the struggling teen, pressing his head hard into the earth. Fassitt screamed out, demanding that the unknown person release him. The tutor now held the collegian fast around the arms, forcing the young man into the light for identification. Suddenly, the hooligan began thrashing the sharp dirk he'd been carrying in his rope belt. Left and right he stabbed blindly behind his back. The tutor relaxed his grip, and the then-unidentified student raced into the night. Dwight walked directly to the North dorm (not North Middle) and the room of a tutor friend, mathematician James Nooney. Blood soaked Dwight's shirt. He told his friend he was badly hurt. The twenty-one-year-old squished across the

Dr. Jonathan Knight, 1789–1864. A leading surgeon in Connecticut and one of the founding professors of Yale's medical college, the doctor was immediately summoned to care for the injured tutor John Breed Dwight. Dr. Knight's testimony would have a crucial impact on the ensuing investigation regarding the attack. This 1827 portrait is by Nathaniel Jocelyn. *Courtesy of Yale University, Harvey Cushing/John Hay Whitney Medical Library.*

room, falling into a chair; his left boot had filled with blood. Dr. Jonathan Knight, from the school's medical college, was summoned and carefully examined Dwight. He'd been struck three times: in front of the groin, in his side and, most severely, in the left hip above the thighbone. One of the incisions came precariously close to the femoral artery. Dwight collapsed unconscious and was placed across the floor.

For three weeks, John Breed Dwight appeared on the mend. During that time, Yale officials quickly and formally expelled Fassitt from the school and chose to keep the assault out of the local papers.[4] However, all was not right with Dwight; feeling well enough to walk outside, he developed a fever and succumbed on October 20,

1843. Dr. Knight determined that the young tutor had actually died from typhoid fever. Later, when questioned by attorneys if the illness were prompted by the stabbing, the physician explained, "It was not one of the ordinary cases of fever resulting from a wound." Then the doctor added, "I do not say there was no connection between the wound and the fever."

Louis Fassitt fled the state. New Haven police officer David Carr pursued the student to Philadelphia, where Fassitt was found hiding in his brother Edward's Washington Square home. That night, the city recorder Richard Vaux authorized the fugitive's arrest and denied bail. However, a group of Fassitt's friends, waving his family's wealthy influence, roused a local judge out of bed, who then proceeded to rescind the recorder's ruling. Bail was allowed at $5,000. Newspapers were incensed. Columns decried the gross miscarriage of justice that had allowed affluence and power to allow a runaway killer his freedom.

On October 23, Fassitt returned to New Haven of his own volition. Accompanied by his father, brother and the abolitionist Presbyterian minister Reverend Albert Barnes (the elder Fassitt was a deacon in the church), the party boarded the mail boat bound for Connecticut. An initial hearing found enough evidence to move the case to trial, set for the upcoming January 1844 session. Bail was reduced to $3,000. On February 1, upon a motion of Fassitt's counsel, the case was continued to the October 1844 term. In mid-October, the defense attorneys moved to quash the indictment on the grounds of improper evidence. During February 1845, the trial was again postponed; Louis's physicians said he was ill and physically incapable of attending court in New Haven. At that juncture, bail was forfeited. Fassitt never returned to Connecticut and never stood trial.

Five years after being expelled from Yale, Louis Fassitt went on to gain a medical degree from the University of Pennsylvania; his final thesis was entitled, "Theory and Art of Prescribing." Fassitt served his internship at Bellevue Hospital in New York City and, afterward, went on to assist the health needs of his Philadelphia community. He died in Englewood, New Jersey, during early December 1883. The public's memory of poor John Breed Dwight quickly dimmed. A couple short biographies appeared in academic journals and then, a mere handful of hourglass sands later, the tutor was sadly forgotten. But strange happenings in North Middle cried out. By the second half of the nineteenth century, the ghostly legacy of the dormitory became an acknowledged facet of Yale tradition.

Physical evidence discovered in the walls of North Middle lends to a theory that another criminal act occurred in or around the dorm. Perhaps it was one of these found objects that enticed a clinging supernatural force.

Relic hunters were excited about the prospect of the ninety-year-old dorm being razed. When demolition commenced in July 1894, laborers carefully combed through the floors, window frames and ceilings in the hope of locating any valuable trinket or hidden treasure. Alumni from around the globe had already placed requests for bricks in the hope of mortaring their own ivied school-day memories. Dozens of bricks bore the initials of long-dead residents, and though the telltale skeleton of North Middle's ghost was not found, some pretty remarkable items quickly surfaced. During the first week or so, a secreted bayonet was revealed in a ground-floor room, two-thirds of a cannon ball was dislodged from the attic's planking and, perhaps most telling of all, a pistol was uncovered. University engineer Charles Barnes was tearing out the gas and water pipes in one of the second floor's front corner rooms when he made this strange find. North Middle's rooms each had a huge recessed closet with double doors (originally they held a primitive murphy bed); there was a four-inch gap between the closet top and the ceiling, along with a slight space between the closet back and the wall. Someone purposely placed this pistol atop the wardrobe and shoved it behind, where the weapon lay hidden for forty years. The barrel was ten inches long and made of the finest steel; the lock was manufactured of heavy brass and the handle carved from ornate mahogany. The weapon's pristine condition astounded the engineer. Barnes noted aloud that the gun looked as if it were "brand new." Apparently it was a dueling pistol. Clearly stamped along its barrel were the words, "New-York, January 1854." Everyone wondered why such a valuable sidearm was discarded. In reality, this weapon may have been a key component in one of the college's darkest storms, the Town and Gown Riots of the 1850s.

The 1854 St. Patrick's Day Riot between Yale students and townies took root as a fracas inside Homan's Athenaeum and came to bloody fruition opposite Trinity Church. The mob wrenched paving stones out of the street and barraged the students, who fired pistols into the frenzy. One rioter was shot through the leg, and an innocent bystander, clockmaker Russell H. Scofield, was hit in the arm. The throng's most vocal ringleader, Patrick O'Neil, grabbed senior John Sims and twice struck him with an iron bar (or, according to another witness, was in the process of strangling the boy). Suddenly, O'Neil crumpled to the pavement. Initially, it was reported that the longshoreman was shot, but as the crowd pulled back allowing the dying man to be escorted to police headquarters, it was determined that the deep wound through the heart was from a knife. The crazed throng, numbering one thousand or more, broke into the armory and stole two cannons, intent on storming the college, while students simultaneously gathered weapons and barricaded themselves in rooms of Brick Row, where, in a medieval mode, they stoked fireplaces preparing hot coals and molten lead to pour down on their rabid attackers. It took all night, but eventually, Police Captain Lyman Bissell, a retired officer from the Mexican War, quelled the insane situation.

John Sims's hat, with his name inside, was recovered where O'Neil had been stabbed, but the individual responsible for the longshoreman's slaying was never identified. The coroner's jury viewed the dead man as an irresponsible agitator, "being at the time engaged in, and leading, aiding, and abetting a riot." The Yale community considered the stabbing a matter of self-defense; students involved in the confrontation refused to answer questions during the coroner's hearing. The matter quickly came to a close.

To avoid further legal complications, or run-ins with the longshoreman's miscreant acquaintances, John Sims (even though he was set to graduate in several weeks) decided it was best to return home to Mississippi. Still, the Sims brothers continued a strong Yale connection. Robert Sims (1838–1886), a member of the Class of 1858, also left school prior to graduation in order to tend the family plantation. A lieutenant in the Confederate army, Robert was wounded at Gettysburg. Captured near the very conclusion of the war, he served the remainder of the conflict in a Union prison. Willie Sims (1842–1891) graduated from Yale in June 1861 and promptly borrowed money from a faculty member to return South, where he also joined the Confederate ranks. William participated in many ferocious battles, suffered from chronic dysentery, was wounded thrice over the course of the war and lost his right foot. He'd become a sorely bitter man over Lee's defeat. Yet Willie was still branded a scalawag Republican by fellow Southerners and compelled to flee his home state, when he accepted unification.

Departing after the Yale Riot, John Sims completed his medical studies in New Orleans. A respected officer in the Confederate army, surgeon Sims rose to the rank of lieutenant colonel, commanding a brigade under General Jubal Early. The Shenandoah was a cursed valley for Yale's rebel

Timothy Dwight V (1828–1916) came from a noble academic lineage. He served as Yale president from 1886 to 1898, and it was during his administration that the institution officially became a university. President Dwight had other plans for the school that had a bearing on Yale hauntings. *From George Rawlinson,* Ancient History, *World's Greatest Classics.*

brothers: Willie Sims was wounded and taken prisoner there in 1864 at the Battle of Cedar Creek. The same bloody fray saw his older sibling, Dr. John Sims, killed.

Brotherly coincidences such as these were tragically an all-too-common part of the Civil War. In a most bizarre and certainly improbable tale, one that seemingly could only spill from the bloody inkwell of Ambrose Bierce, the *New York Sun* on the eve of Halloween 1887 reported that after the Battle of Cedar Creek, officers gathered about a campfire relating thoughts of the fight and the next day's strategies. The conversation, for some reason, swelled old memories within Dr. Sims of the long-ago Yale Riot. Gazing into the flaming logs, the lieutenant colonel shared, perhaps for the first time, how he, in the course of being throttled, defended himself with a dirk, felling his assailant. At that moment, Sims himself suddenly crumpled to the ground, the lone peel of a gunshot reverberating far off in the darkness. Positioned a quarter mile away, a Union sharpshooter was ordered to take aim at the rebel blaze. No one realized until some years later that the soldier squeezing the trigger was the brother of Patrick O'Neil, the man Sims had stabbed in front of Trinity Church a decade earlier.

Whatever passing strange episodes plagued North Middle, no living soul can say. Was the ghost the earthbound spirit of a tutor, or was the specter hinged to the site by a weapon fired during a riot's hateful commotion? Perhaps a Southern family's grief hundreds of miles away spawned an energy that carried a dead man back to his last place of innocence. The destruction of North Middle would ultimately release this lonely apparition; definitely the room most associated with the death of tutor Dwight, apartment eighty-four, was erased from the face of the earth when the building came down. Ironically, a true story concerning a brother's revenge would never make the newspapers. The man responsible for the razing of Yale's Old Brick Row was the university president Timothy Dwight V, the younger brother of tutor John Breed Dwight.

## Chapter 4

# The Sea Captain, the Alchemist and the Magic Codex

## New Haven's Very Own Robinson Crusoe

*We knew nothing where we were, or upon what land it was we were driven,*
*whether an island or the main, whether inhabited or not inhabited; and as the rage*
*of the wind was still great, though rather less than at first, we could not so much*
*as hope to have the ship hold many minutes without breaking in pieces.*
Robinson Crusoe
*Daniel Defoe, 1719*

Few recall how the calm waters of New Haven Harbor gave screeching life to one of the New World's greatest tales of survival: the miraculous shipwreck of Ephraim Howe and Nicholas Augur in the autumn of 1676. The adventures of these two New Haven men were first preserved during the final quarter of the seventeenth century by some long-forgotten minister-scholar as part of a collated quest for the supernatural. The history of this strange story is itself buried deep within the realm of magic and religion.

One of New England's most influential Puritan leaders was Increase Mather (1639–1723). The mystic-historian uncovered a rather peculiar manuscript in John Davenport's immense library. Davenport, the Puritan founder of New Haven, had been amassing paranormal stories and recently taken up residence in Boston. Mather's intrigue with this vast collection of marvels compelled the Boston leader to bring Davenport's unique library to the attention of New England ministers in 1681, eleven years after Davenport's death. All agreed to continue the research and to expand the tales initially embraced by the New Haven reverend. The resulting expansive

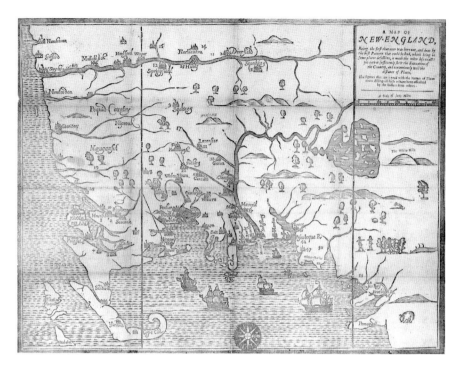

Resembling a strange chart from a Tolkien book, this is actually the first map ever published in New England. It depicts the coast Howe routinely sailed and was engraved during the time the New Haven seafarer confronted his horrific ordeals. The Puritan outpost of New Haven can be seen in the farthest reaches of this wonderful map. *A Map of New England.* *"White Hills" version. Woodcut, printed by John Foster, 1677. Originally published in* A Narrative of the Troubles with the Indians *by William Hubbard (Boston: printed by John Foster, 1677). Courtesy of the Massachusetts Historical Society.*

tome was a declaration of supernatural events occurring in early New England. Credited to Increase Mather, the book was entitled *An Essay for the Recording of Illustrious Providences* and was first published in Boston during 1684. The age-tainted pages offer a detailed potion of New England apparitions, demons, witchcraft, strange weather phenomenon and ocean-borne miracles. The tragic saga of New Haven sailor Ephraim Howe first unfurled its sails in the pages of this magic codex. So incredible are Howe's experiences that Cotton Mather (the son of Increase) brought the New Haven sailor's journey back to life in his own book, *Magnalia Christi Americana* in 1702.

Passages inside these velum works were not tales of "the unexplained" but rather, within the Puritan mind, stories that provided "the explanation" of God's existence and will: "Puritan's viewed all extraordinary events as providential in their expression of God's power and purpose. They believed that wonders revealed not only God's ascendency over the world, but also his attitude toward humanity at the moment when the wonder occurred...For that reason, Puritans were eager to record and digest all supernatural incidents, and to ponder their significance."[5]

This skipper's sufferings spawned dark circles under the eyes of sea-going men for generations. Beginning in about 1800, Howe's story was republished roughly once each decade in maudlin mariner's chronicles and shipwreck narratives. Times changed, but the sea did not. To antebellum America, a nation of whalers and fisheries, these newer books aimed to exploit the misery of the sailor's lot, with nary a spyglass glance toward

Increase Mather (1639–1723) discovered a manuscript of notable and supernatural stories in the library of Reverend John Davenport. Later, Mather and a number of New England ministers expanded this collection and entitled the work, *An Essay For the Recording of Illustrious Providences* (published in 1684). *Courtesy Bridgeport Public Library.*

the miraculous. Puritan meditations devolved into pure sensationalism. Nevertheless, Increase and Cotton Mathers's miracles remain. This particular wonder-tale, born in New Haven, will continue to return with the tide, for those willing to believe.

---

Most everyone is aware of Daniel Defoe's early eighteenth-century castaway Robinson Crusoe. Many scholars agree that this fictional character was likely inspired by the true-life daring of Alexander Selkirk, who was marooned in the South Pacific. However, another influence Defoe could have drawn from, particularly with regard to the novel's religious motifs, was Ephraim Howe, whose survival adventure was considered truly supernatural.

Howe was a hardworking New Haven sailor familiar to everyone along the New England coast. Faces brightened whenever they saw the captain's name, spelled "How" in its Old World manner, mentioned with that day's ship arrivals.

The fifty-year-old skipper was born north of London, in Hatfield, Broadoak, Essex, England, in about 1626. Young Ephraim and his siblings became part of "the Great Migration" of Puritans when his family arrived in the Massachusetts Bay Colony aboard the *Truelove* during late November 1635. Edward, his father, was a respected gentleman who quickly acquired land but sadly died, just three and a half years after venturing to New England. About the age of twenty-five, Ephraim married Ann Haugh in Lynn, Massachusetts. Within a couple years, Ephraim and his wife moved south to the Puritan stronghold of New Haven.

Captain Howe routinely sailed north, transporting letters, small bundles and passengers between his home and Boston. Yet no one could have foretold the torments about to strangle the captain and his shipmates as they stepped on the gangplank of his two-masted ketch on August 25, 1676.

There were a total of six onboard. Howe sailed with a crew of three, two of his sons (records are contradictory regarding which of Ephraim's four sons—Ephraim Jr., Samuel, Daniel or Isaac—were actually with their father) and a cabin boy, who surely cooked and scrubbed the galley. Also onboard were two prestigious New Haven colonists, Nicholas Augur and Caleb Jones.

---

Beginning in 1643, Nicholas Augur's name became associated with some of New Haven Colony's earliest records. When Thomas Pell, New Haven's first doctor moved to Westchester County, New York, during 1654, Augur took his place, thus becoming the second doctor to practice in New Haven. Granted a home lot "reserved for an elder" fronting the Green, his residence was situated on what we today recognize as the southeast corner of Church and Elm Streets. Augur most likely learned his trade as an apprentice. Lacking academic training, he became schooled in remedies by observing an experienced practitioner, while helping to mix potions and herbal cures. Armed with lancet and poultice, Mr. Augur confronted the colony's long-standing battle with "ague and fever," or what we today call malarial fever.[6]

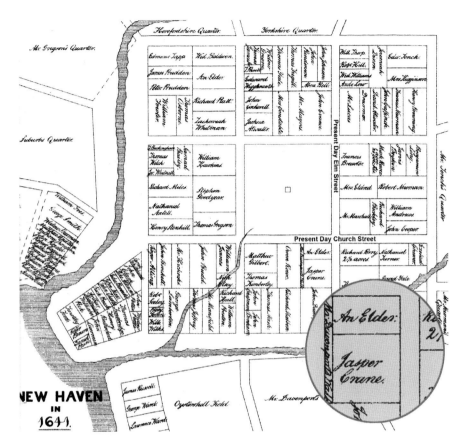

The 1641 John Brockett *Map of New Haven* illustrates the town's original nine squares. When Nicholas Augur became the colony's second ever physician, he was provided a home opposite the center square's "market place." The location is labeled as the property of "An Elder" and situated where Elm and Church Streets intersect today. *Courtesy of the Connecticut State Library.*

In fact, there were any number of "fevers" in those colonial days, beyond smallpox, measles and diphtheria.

The poor looked fondly on Augur. He was known to have "given phisicke" to both servants as well as "to a mare that was bitten wth a rattell snake."[7] Civic minded as well, just six months prior to setting sail with Howe, a rumor began circulating that the Narragansetts planned to attack New Haven. The doctor donated money to help construct a protective palisade surrounding the Puritan enclave.

The good doctor also owned a dark nook in the frightful annals of New England's witch hysteria, which had a firm hold on seventeenth-century

Fear of Connecticut's foreboding woods contributed to the witchcraft hysteria of the seventeenth century well before Salem's witch trials. Between 1653 and 1689 six people (one of them twice) were dragged before New Haven courts to answer accusations concerning dealings with Satan. Nicholas Augur examined women seemingly afflicted by diabolic spells and brought his findings to the notice of highly regarded physician John Winthrop Jr. *Illustration from Joseph Glanvill.* Saducismus triumphatus: Or, a Full and Plain Evidence, Concerning Witches and Apparitions..

Connecticut. In 1653, Elizabeth Godman stood before a court in order to respond to charges connecting her to a variety of supernatural crimes. These included casting spells that caused illness and death of children and livestock, clairvoyance and the wholly unsavory act of allowing the devil to suckle her breast. In jestful contempt, it was Elizabeth Godman herself who propagated this last lurid debauchery. Three local woman—Mary Bishop, Elizabeth Brewster and Hannah Lamberton—collapsed into terrifying fits after confronting the strangely babbling Widow Godman. Attempting to diagnose these seizures by consulting a university-trained physician, as was the custom of the day, Dr. Augur sent a correspondence to John Winthrop Jr., a resident of Pequot (present-day New London). Oddly enough, while detailing the supernatural "disease" afflicting his three female patients, Augur concluded his letter by stating that the bouts of convulsions immediately vanished when the magistrates examined accused witch Elizabeth Godman.[8]

Despite his dedication to fellow townspeople, records attest to the fact that the doctor was often in court demanding that his patients pay their bills. Augur's mystical research and approach to medicine caused another problem. Some within the colony did not care for the treatments he recommended and continually petitioned other physicians to take up local residence. The reality is that his medical colleagues couldn't have provided an

Son of the first governor of Massachusetts, John Winthrop the younger founded New London with the vision of establishing a Puritan-Alchemist bastion of learning. Before becoming governor of the Connecticut Colony in 1657, he lived in New Haven for two years. During this time he supplanted Nichols Augur's practice as local healer. *Illustration from Charles Mackay.* Extraordinary Popular Delusions and the Madness of Crowds. *London: Office of the National Illustrated Library, 1852.*

iota of additional cure; beyond bleeding patients, Augur and his misguided and superstitious counterparts merely prescribed an assortment of "boiled toads, eels, and other unsavory and nauseating materials" to be churned into horrible mixtures for consumption.[9]

In the face of such volatile employment situations, Augur and his kindred New England alchemists actively hedged against financial uncertainty by pursuing simultaneous divergent business enterprises. The doctor was also a New Haven merchant with extensive dealings requiring visits to Plymouth and Boston. These frequent trips were quite hazardous. Any seventeenth-century sea voyage carried, along with its cargo, the dire reality of drowning, wreck or Indian attack. Ever the businessman, Augur drafted his last will and testament prior to a 1673 coastal jaunt. The doctor-merchant named his sister the sole beneficiary.

Not much is known about the remaining passenger, Caleb Jones. His memory is overshadowed by the life of his illustrious father, William, a magistrate. For decades, the powerful man had served in a variety of lofty posts, including deputy governor for the colony of New Haven. However, besides his association with skipper Howe, Caleb holds a special place in New Haven history. Namely, the possibility that years earlier, young Caleb may have met the regicides Whalley and Goffe, those legendary figures who had signed the death sentence of Charles I. While avoiding the king's soldiers, the regicides were secreted in the Jones's New Haven home. Caleb's own grandfather was regicide John Jones.

After discharging his cargo in Boston, skipper Howe, the crew and the same two passengers—Augur and Jones—set out for the return trip to Connecticut on September 10, 1676. Contrary winds proved too much for the vessel, and the ketch was forced back into the harbor.

Tragically for Ephraim and all of Boston's citizens, the settlement at the time was wrestling with the shroud and sickle of the "bloody flux." This was

Ephraim Howe piloted this type of small vessel during a violent North Atlantic storm. His passengers tied him to the helm, where he stood for thirty-six-hour intervals. *Courtesy of George L. Clark, A History of Connecticut: Its People and Institutions.*

the seventeenth-century appellation applied to the water and food-borne disease we now recognize as dysentery. Boston's epidemic of 1676 saw many dying from the "grippings, vomiting, and flux and fever" of this illness.

Following a month of shudder and vomit, skipper Howe once again attempted to board his vessel. Though wearied, Ephraim felt certain that the day's fair wind boded well. The journey home should not tax his health further, and he sorely missed his wife, Ann. On October 10 (today's calendar equivalent is October 22), he pointed the prow of his ship southward toward New Haven. But the weather took a decided, though sudden, turn within view of Cape Cod.

For some reason, God frowned on Howe. A monstrous storm was clawing its way up the Atlantic.[10] Towering waves came smashing down on the small ship. Manacled to the thrashing ogre's whims, the ketch was dragged far out to sea. Soaked to the bone and lacking sleep, Ephraim's son became seriously ill. Perhaps while in Boston, he too had contracted the bloody flux. Whatever the reason, it was during their eleventh day inside the storm that the young man died. With little more ceremony than a shouted prayer thrown into the teeth of the howling torrent, the young man was cast overboard. Much to the superstitious bent of both sailors and Puritans, Ephraim pondered what sins he had committed to deserve such a fate. Matters worsened. Shortly after the loss of his one son, Ephraim's other boy expired. A hell-borne situation grew fangs. The only man left capable of managing the ketch was skipper Howe. Following the captain's desperate orders, passengers Jones and Augur wrestled with the roaring ocean. Holding fast to the heaving deck, they gathered all the rope at hand and lashed Howe to the helm.

The demon sea obliterated time. Hours, days and weeks roiled into a seamless nightmare. Howe struggled at the rudder for periods of up to thirty-six straight hours. Succumbing to exhaustion, Caleb Jones perished. There was no need to lower Caleb's remains into the water. His lifeless body jumbled to and fro along the deck's planks while the sea rose and hungrily swallowed the corpse. Then, there were three. The captain, Augur and the cabin boy.

Withered by labor and sleeplessness, Captain Howe asked the doctor to pray with him and humbly ask what direction God might wish them to attempt: the New England coast or the West Indies. They drew lots that decided the outcome: New England. By this time, it was November 10—they had been a month at sea. The ocean and storm had caused tremendous stress on the vessel, and the rudder was lost. Directionless, the ship bobbed along the heedless waves for two weeks. The men lay lethargic on the deck. Early in the morning, about November 24, they were startled awake by the sound of roaring breakers. Pulling themselves up to peer over the gunwales, they witnessed how close their vessel had come to crashing and sinking on a submerged ledge. In the distance, a miracle loomed: an island. Dropping anchor, they shouted thankfulness to God. If the breakers had not warned them, they would have missed the island as well as been dashed to splinters on the rocks.

Author Daniel Defoe's fictional character Robinson Crusoe (imaginatively depicted here) was based on the life of Alexander Selkirk. The 1719 novel also relates to the woeful tale of New Haven sailor Ephraim Howe. *Illustration from* The Life and Strange Surprising Adventures of Robinson Crusoe…, *by Daniel Defoe, London, 1863.*

Now another miracle: the sea was calmed by the hand of the Almighty. As swiftly as their broken bodies would allow, they lowered the lifeboat. Damaged boards proved the tiny craft unseaworthy. Seeing that it wasn't safe to stow any of the ship's stores, they dragged themselves into the little boat, carrying only the clothes on their backs and their firearms. Straining at the oars, they eventually made landfall. It was a barren beach. Gazing up and down the shore, Howe, Augur and the cabin boy saw only rock and salt spray. Without knowing, they stood on a spit of ledge on the southernmost tip of Nova Scotia, not far from Cape Sable. Their new home was a desolate locale sailors still speak of as the graveyard of the Atlantic. But by almighty God, they rejoiced—it was land.

As benevolent as Providence was for this moment, the storm soon returned with renewed fury. The ketch, still at anchor some distance from the island, was splintered and sank. Staggering luck, however, resulted in a handful of precious items washing ashore:

A cask of gunpowder (somehow it had survived the saltwater).
One barrel of wine.
Half a barrel of molasses.
Several yards of sturdy cloth.

It was late November on the North Atlantic coast. Without trees or other natural barriers, the cold blasts and frigid weather became an enormous hazard. The three castaways erected a rude tent with the materials on hand. Then, hunger arrived. Although the men were armed, the island offered little game other than scattered crows, ravens and gulls. Half of one of the scrawny birds with a mouthful of wine made for a whole day's meal; there was a five-day period when the shipwreck victims did not eat a morsel. The men subsisted on prayer and scavenging during the bitter winter, all the while Ephraim notched a stick to count the gaunt days. The cut-marks added up to weeks. It was then mid-February 1677. After so many coastal voyages together and having survived three months in their wretched situation, skipper Howe's dear friend Dr. Augur died. Now only the boy and captain felt the bite of wind and gnaw of hunger.

Roughly a month and a half later, on April 2, 1677, the cabin boy, too, passed away. Captain Howe was alone. Sole ruler of that rock-strewn universe, he was left to wander the shore to and fro watching the horizon. On several occasions, Howe's spirits soared with the sight of a fishing vessel. The skipper stoked a smoky distress signal. Tears filled his weather-cracked face when the boats merely sailed by, abandoning Howe's lonely shrieks to join the few miserable squawking gulls. To Howe, it was unthinkable that these crews could have possibly missed his signal fires. Most likely those sailors decided to avoid the island, fearing an ambush from Wampanoag, Nipmuck or Narragansett warriors still fighting King Phillip's War.[11]

After surviving the bloody flux, losing his two sons and a close friend, being lost at sea and then shipwrecked and starving on a barren island, Ephraim fell to his knees, not in despair but in thankfulness. As tenaciously as Howe had battled for life, he reverently thanked God for the gifts bestowed on him throughout his long ordeal. Ephraim looked toward heaven and shouted: despite sickness and sea-wreck, abandon and hunger, by God's will, he alone had survived.

Not long after Howe's sacred testimonial, a Salem

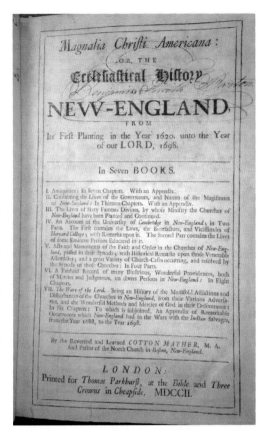

*Magnalia Christi Americana.* The Latin title translates to "Glorious Works of Christ in America." Written by Cotton Mather (1663–1728) and published in 1702, its seven sections, or "books," examine the preternatural mysteries of New England, including the Salem witch trials and Ephraim Howe's shipwreck. *Courtesy of Elihu Burritt Library, Central Connecticut State University. Photograph by Matthew Bielawa.*

trading brig approached his lonely home. A boat was lowered and rowed toward the smoke of Ephraim's watch fire. Savage in his appearance, wearing only rags, Howe embraced the sailors. The crew shared broth; Ephraim shared his tale. On July 18, 1677, the vessel put into Salem-town. Following bedridden days needed to gather his stamina, Ephraim Howe returned home to New Haven. It was late August 1677. Like brave Ulysses, shriveled, aged and with a vaguely familiar visage, he entered his home.

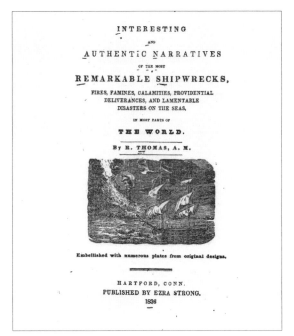

INTERESTING
AND
AUTHENTIC NARRATIVES
OF THE MOST
REMARKABLE SHIPWRECKS,
FIRES, FAMINES, CALAMITIES, PROVIDENTIAL
DELIVERANCES, AND LAMENTABLE
DISASTERS ON THE SEAS,
IN MOST PARTS OF
THE WORLD.
By R. THOMAS, A. M.

Embellished with numerous plates from original designs.

HARTFORD, CONN.
PUBLISHED BY EZRA STRONG.
1836

The harrowing adventures of New Haven's Ephraim Howe were celebrated in mariners' chronicles for nearly a century following father and son Mather's wonder-books. The tale's initial miraculous moral transformed into a rugged survival tale thrilling generations of schoolboys and sailors. *Courtesy Michael J. Bielawa Collection.*

Most certainly his wife, Ann, swooned with the site of this doorway ghost. It was a year since Howe's departure from New Haven.

With a notion to escape the sea's tentacles, skipper Howe moved inland. And just as Robinson Crusoe contemplated with his closing lines, Ephraim, too, most certainly thought, "I am preparing for a longer journey."

Indeed, the trauma he endured shortened the sailor's life. Ephraim Howe would die, in Wallingford, Connecticut, three years after his miraculous resurrection from the sea.

*Chapter 5*

# His Strange Majesty

## The Monarch of East Rock

*Sailors coming in from a voyage cross themselves when they first see it, and the old Yankees believe it would be a much graver matter than death to climb it, if indeed that were possible. Nevertheless there is an ancient house on that cliff, and at evening men see lights in the small-paned windows.*
*"The Strange High House in the Mist"*
*H.P. Lovecraft, 1926*

*As they ascended, Rip every now and then heard long rolling peals, like distant thunder, that seemed to issue out of a deep ravine, or rather cleft, between lofty rocks.*
*"Rip Van Winkle"*
*Washington Irving, 1819*

Two hundred million years ago, the region we recognize today as New Haven was a violent mass of molten rock. Lava erupted and churned as the supercontinent Pangaea ripped apart. Eons of cooling and weathering eventually formed the trap-rock ridges now enclosing New Haven. Running east to west, this series of promontory palisades are known as East Rock, Mill Rock, Pine Rock and West Rock. The stony land might appear solid, but these summits stir with strange events and bizarre inhabitants. Presciently, when the Dutch explorers first spied East Rock's ruddy crest, they dubbed the locale *Rodenberg*, or "Red Mountain," for its hue: the color of blood.

Enchanted by dense woods and daunting terrain, some hearty early American outcasts chose to make these rusty mountains their lofty lairs. Like

Upon viewing the towering reddish ledge, the first Dutch explorers named this area *Rodenberg*, or "Red Mountain." The lonely cliffs would host many lost souls who turned their backs on humanity. This scene depicts East Rock as it appeared in 1858. Careful scrutiny brings into faint focus the former residence of the Smith family who were brutally murdered. *Courtesy of the New Haven Museum Photo Archives.*

his Old Testament namesake, one of the earliest New Haven hermits was called Elias. Townsfolk were readily aware of Elias Turner, who frequented the lowlands, bartering kindling and herbs. The ragged man created quite a scene walking beside his little wagon drawn by a team of baying sheep. During lean frigid months, the hermit silently waited on city doorsteps accepting whatever morsels residents were willing to bestow.

The mystique of New Haven's hermit was celebrated by Henry Collins Flagg.[12] As editor of the weekly *Connecticut Herald*, Flagg emulated the Romantic notion of Washington Irving's fictional Hudson Valley chronicler, Dutch historian Diedrich Knickerbocker. Under the pseudonym Jeremy Broadcloth, Flagg described an 1821 visit to the East Rock hermit:

> *We found him on the top of the mountain, in the midst of a thick wood. He was seated on a stone, stirring the expiring embers of a fire, which had been kindled in the hollow of an old stump. His dress consisted of a loose farmer's frock and trowsers [sic] of the coarsest materials. A leather cap, which seemed a scalp, was the only covering of his head…Believing that the poor wretch was absolutely demented, we prepared to return [to New Haven]; when I proposed to look for some spring to quench my thirst. Without appearing to notice us, the Hermit rose, and proceeded to a small inclosure [sic] of stonework, which composed a rude cabin, and an apology*

*for a court yard. He entered the walls, and soon held up a bottle of water,
to the neck of which a long string was attached.*

Turner's kind act was possible due to a well he had dug with seashells. As for
the interior of the cabin, Edward Atwater noted in his 1887 *History of the City of
New Haven to the Present Day*, "The hut was about twelve feet square and partly
underground." His sooty hovel was built of earth and stone, with the entrance
doubling as a chimney. His bed was composed of tree boughs and corn husks.

A favorite target for badgering youngsters, the hermit allowed himself to
be lured into a State Street shop one day during 1822. Mr. Blakeslee, the
proprietor, enjoyed mocking the bearded fellow as much as the boys and
bet the hermit that if he could drink a quart of Santa Cruz rum, the store
owner would pay for the bottle. Everyone at the long counter nudged one
another and laughed as Turner accepted the wager. The hermit was no fool,
however. He purchased a loaf of bread and, by soaking large pieces in the
alcohol, ate the jug of rum.

Elias's primitive lifestyle took its toll. On November 2, 1823, the hermit
of East Rock was found dead in his semiunderground hut. The cause was
officially noted as "a visitation from God." The coroner found forty dollars
in silver carefully sewn inside the lining of the hermit's patchwork trousers.

Two years after Elias's death, John Turvell Adams published a poem
entitled the "Hermit of East Rock." Already a part of contemporary New
Haven folklore, the verse wrestles with the hermit's decision to remove
himself from humanity:

*I do remember an old man, that once,*
*For some years, on that crag made his abode,*
*And hence was named, "The Hermit of East Rock"…*

*…Respecting his estrangement from the world;*
*But they were only visions of romance:*
*The secret of his grief is in his grave…*

*The sorrows of the wretched man were o'er.*
*His spirit had departed, and alone,*
*As he had lived, so did he die, alone.*[13]

In addition to hermit Turner's hidden silver, other treasures have been
discovered on East Rock. No one knows for certain who secreted the 1833

cache that two hunters stumbled on tucked inside a tree. A crumbling canvas pouch contained several hundred dollars, jewelry, papers and a pair of eyeglasses. One of the documents, a bill, included the name "Charles Foote, Bridgeport" (consulting the United States Census indicated that a fellow by that same name was living in Bridgeport during 1830). Decades later, in 1886, an indentation located halfway down the face of the rust-toned mountain exposed a cave. Extending fifteen feet inward, it was littered with arrowheads and a couple early American coins, dated 1785 and 1792. The locale may have housed a forgotten drifter so common on the rock. It seems a strange tradition was born with Turner's hidden silver. In addition to wandering souls, East Rock became associated with buried treasure. Greed for lost loot would entice a coldblooded murderer to the rock and ultimately bring to the mountain its most famous hermit.

Those spirited Dutch explorers who once called out "Rodenberg" most certainly marooned some of their olden legends on East Rock. Like the ghostly Dutch gnomes at their thunderous bowling games in the neighboring "Kaatskill" Mountains, a malevolent peal also rumbled among the crevasses of New Haven's red peak.

In the early 1840s, Elizur Hubbell constructed a tourist retreat at the rock's summit. He named the stone edifice the Mountain House and offered food, drink and majestic views as well as a ten-pin alley for recreation. Hubbell's tourist venture lasted a mere five years, from 1843 to 1848. But the supernatural growls of a rolling ball and crashing ectoplasmic pins would continue to mingle with the dark forest laughter of wild-eyed hermits.

The next inhabitants on the jutting crest, Charles and Ann Smith, like the reclusive Turner, would soon be claimed by the mountain. The elderly couple optimistically relocated to the lonely Mountain House after Hubbell's business failure. The sixty-seven-year-old Charles was born in Warwickshire, England, and had fought beside the Duke of Wellington during the Napoleonic Wars. Tired of the Old World's battles and instability, the Smiths had crossed the Atlantic for New England's calm. Atop East Rock, the Smiths continued to operate the bowling alley. It was during the autumn of 1849 that a stranger to New Haven, James McCaffrey, hiked up the mountain to inquire about purchasing the Smiths' retreat. McCaffrey liked the business opportunities that the East Rock property provided. Ann set another plate on the table. She stirred a pot of cabbage over the fireplace while corned beef simmered beneath the lid of another kettle. In the glow of the hot embers, Mrs. Smith grinned about the future while Charles and the speculator strolled outside discussing a selling price.

Neighbors at the base of the rock became concerned when the couple failed to appear in town for their weekly errands. "Maybe they were ill," folks worried. Venturing up to the stone house, friends found a table set for three. Obviously, they reasoned, a guest had been expected. But the food and chimney coals were cold. Searchers called aloud, but the couple was nowhere to be found—until four days later. Ann Smith was discovered in the brush, just off the ridge trail, her garments caked in blood; the sixty-three-year-old woman had been shot through the heart. War veteran Charles was found a bit farther along the same path, wounded in the stomach. It was evident that he had struggled and been finally killed by the blow of a rock to the head. Evidence soon implicated James McCaffrey. The broad-shouldered stranger owned a double-barrel pistol and had been witnessed drinking at local saloons with Smith on the day of the murder. In McCaffrey's haste to abandon New Haven by train, he had left a trunk behind. Concealed within his clothing was a bullet-casting device. Police consulted an expert gunsmith and found that the slug removed from Mrs. Smith fit the mold. After a four-month chase, the culprit was finally apprehended in Canada. When McCaffrey returned to New Haven for trial, prosecutors detailed how he had killed the couple and then searched for a treasure he was certain they had hidden on the mountain. McCaffrey was convicted and executed for the murder of Ann Smith on October 2, 1850.

With its brambles and whispering weeds, the abandoned Smith house cultivated a sinister reputation. Attempting to exorcise the demons on the mountaintop, someone purposely set fire to the stone structure. The ruins were avoided by townspeople, except for vagrants seeking to escape inclement weather. One vagabond, however, refused to believe (or perhaps, readily embraced) the tales of East Rock ghosts. The hermit Milton Stewart resided within the ruins over a longer course of time than any of his fellow transients. Eventually, Stewart claimed squatter's rights for not just the charred building but also most of the mountain.

The man who would be monarch of East Rock was born in New Hampshire about the year 1822. He was a carpenter by trade, some said he worked in a shipyard, prior to relocating to the mountain's brow just a handful of years before the Civil War. As if challenging the mountain

The ever-enterprising Milton Stewart built this refreshment stand for folks visiting his personal mountain. Those found hiking on East Rock without permission of the Monarch were charged a toll of ten cents—at gunpoint. *Courtesy of the New Haven Museum Photo Archives.*

spirits, East Rock's newest hermit expanded the gutted Smith place stone by stone with his own hands. His two-story mansion cut through the woods at rambling angles, creating a freakish appearance. It was the perfect haunt for a madman. The hermit was a flurry of zealous activity; at some point, he constructed a stone refreshment stand for mountain visitors. In addition to chopping trees and working the quarry, the monarch of East Rock built a long stretch of stairs leading up the face of his kingdom.

His most well-known, and bizarre, construction project attracted endless guffaws. It was quite a surprising sight when visitors encountered a ship on top of a mountain. Miles from the nearest water, the rough hull was held aloft on sawhorses, wooden barrels and felled trees. Stewart christened the forty-foot vessel *Above the Clouds*. Locals jokingly preferred "Stewart's Steamboat." Built of East Rock timber, cut and hewn by Stewart himself, the steam-driven ship featured a novel smokestack "on hinges" to accommodate for low bridge spans. Cap'n Milton envisioned selling tickets, a hundred passengers at a time, for excursions on Long Island Sound. As crazy sounding as a wild-haired Claus Kinski, this reverse "Fitzcarraldo" made careful calculations to deforest a swath of East Rock and move the craft down from the summit on skids during winter. But the ship was too bulky and heavy. A nest of cables and pulleys never worked either. So there the ship sat, on top of East Rock. In keeping with all his absurd plans, the hull eventually became a sort of gigantic stationary message in a bottle. Visitors looking for the monarch of East Rock tacked notes to the hull. In the evenings, Milton Stewart would read each letter and post his reply back on the ship's side.

Throughout his reign atop East Rock, people questioned Stewart's sanity. For one thing, he would wander the stone face with his dog and shotgun seeking hikers. Once, he even threatened visitors with a raised ax. Whenever he found these scenery-loving "trespassers," he demanded that they pay a toll of ten cents; incredulous, visitors would balk, "What for?" Stewart would flatly reply, "For my view." There was another reason Stewart carried a weapon: the remote site attracted unsavory and sometimes violent characters. His wife, Annie (who first came to East Rock around 1863–1864), had been raped on the Hamden side of the mountain during late June 1882.

Politicians long sought to evict the troublesome monarch from his stone mansion. When plans came together to create an East Rock Park, city fathers rubbed their anxious hands, drooling over prospects for the ruddy mountain. Condemning Stewart's property, the city declared eminent domain and paid the miffed squatter $13,000. Always combative, Stewart squandered most of the money in an unwinnable three-year legal battle to take back the mountain. In early 1883, he stormed off East Rock for the last time and, according to popular legend, sought revenge on the city. Stewart assumed a strategy of deplorable high-jinx. For example, the deposed monarch of the rock partially buried a dead mule on a public road at the base of the mountain. Aside from being halfheartedly concealed in dirt and rubbish, the carcass was readily visible by one of its legs sticking straight up; the calling card of a man's hat was left dangling on the exposed hoof.

But it was Stewart's State Street construction project that raised a worse stench. With the money remaining from the city's $13,000 buyout, he acquired a tract of swampland and hastily assembled twelve tenement buildings. Neighbors shook their heads. The homes' street-side fronts appeared straight and sturdy enough, but the weight of the buildings was supported by flimsy pilings rammed into the marsh. Dubbed the "Dirt Dozen" and "Stewart's Folly" (a witty play on words sarcastically referring to Secretary of State William H. Seward's own mocked purchase of Alaska), half of the homes were immediately condemned as unsafe.

The monarch's original legacy was faring no better. Back on top of East Rock, what was left standing of the shattered Stewart Mansion after

The Dirty Dozen. Looking down from East Rock, in the center of this photograph, are twelve identical homes situated tightly in a row. When city fathers wrestled the reddish pinnacle from Milton Stewart's grasp, they gave him $13,000. The deposed monarch used the money to construct these ill-fated tenements on swampland. *Courtesy of the New Haven Museum Photo Archives.*

Eccentric Milton Stewart claimed squatter's rights when he inhabited an abandoned stone house atop East Rock. Over time, he expanded the place into a foreboding castlelike structure. When the building was razed in 1884, mysterious tunnels and secret rooms were discovered. This image is taken from an undated stereographic card. Popular during the nineteenth century, these cards utilized dual photo technology to create a 3D image of famous sites and attractions. *Courtesy of the New Haven Museum Photo Archives.*

hoodlums had moved in and ransacked the place was razed in 1884. During the work, a surprised holler caused the demolition crew to gaze down into the shifting debris. A trapdoor was revealed in the kitchen corner. The hatch led to a secret tunnel, three feet wide and tall enough for a man to stand in, that ran roughly forty feet beneath the floor. Construction workers pacing the secret passageway discovered it had once run even farther, seeing that it terminated at a portion of the foundation covered with concrete. Another underground hidden chamber was found: a room measuring ten feet square and seven feet in height. Adding to the mystery, a broken metal die and two counterfeit bills were discovered on the dust-laden floor. Monarch Stewart denied any knowledge of the tunnel or room.

Milton Stewart died in the summer of 1897. A few months later, banks foreclosed on the remaining "Dirty Dozen" tenements. As for the boat left stranded atop the rock, the park association grabbed the last laugh. It converted the vessel into a humongous flowerpot.

Strange stories haunted the Monarch of East Rock, even after his death. Around the time this 1900 photograph was taken, rumors circulated in newspapers across the nation that Milton Stewart was building an ark on top of East Rock due to an impending apocalyptic flood. The roof of the refreshment stand pokes above the trees at the mountain's edge, and the mighty Soldiers and Sailors Monument (dedicated in 1887) towers in the center. *Courtesy of the New Haven Museum Photo Archives.*

In a bizarre turn of events, the deceased eccentric's voice continued to pontificate from his throne on East Rock. In 1899, two years after Stewart's death, newspapers across the nation sensationally announced that his ship, *Above the Clouds*, was being built by a very much alive monarch, who, with a nod to Noah, was planning to rescue a handful of faithful New Havenites from the impending Armageddon of 1900. Although dead and buried, Stewart was readily quoted in papers such as the *New Orleans Daily Picayune* about the soon-to-be-realized flood: "I believe that the wickedness which has made the United States degenerate morally will assuredly be punished. I am positive that the Almighty will roll the waters of the Atlantic and the Pacific upon this broad country [during the summer of 1900], and that every acre of land will be completely inundated...Our cities [will] be washed away by the mighty rush of waters, [leaving] only ruins where once proud cities stood."

Though the foreseen deluge never occurred, East Rock itself provides a spectacular flood of sorts. Cast your eyes on this reddish Gibraltar rising from Connecticut's core. Legends continually flow down from its amber ridge. Torrents of history cascade from its caves, secret ruins and treasures, inundating New Haven. The true monarch of this mountain is its ceaseless fountain of the majestic and the mysterious.

*Chapter 6*

# The Final Chantey of
# New England's Last Pirate

*I strike for the memory of long-vanished years:*
*I only shed blood where another sheds tears.*
*I come, as the lightening comes red from above,*
*O'er the race that I loathe, to the battle I love.*
*Pirate's Song, anonymous*

*They can hang me, I don't care, for my revenge will be sweet.*
*William Delaney, alias the Red Pirate*

The long and bloodcurdling line of New England–born pirates ended its
gory legacy right here on the shores of New Haven. And not so far back
as one might think. William Delaney, otherwise known as the Red Pirate and
Cast Iron Bill, was born in the Elm City on April 15, 1851. (Not without
irony, the multifaceted sea-robber was accompanied into this world with
Herman Melville's soul-assaulting novel about tortured Ahab and outcast
Ishmael.) For better or worse, and city fathers surely felt the worse, wherever
adventure carried the Long Wharf swashbuckler, buccaneer Delaney never
failed to dampen the reputation of New Haven when he haughtily claimed
the city his beloved home.

During an all-too-brief and supremely tragic life, the Red Pirate proudly
shouted his birthplace to everyone within earshot or pistol range, splashing
his nativity in ink across whale-ship papers and pounding a grog-grasping
New Haven fist on tavern tables around the world; and when his passion for

William Delaney, alias the Red Pirate and Cast Iron Bill, was born in New Haven far after the golden age of piracy. But once, New England had been teaming with freebooters such as the Rhode Island pirate Thomas Tew, who may have plundered under the flag pictured here. Cast Iron Bill would have been welcome in the company of such buccaneers. *Courtesy Michael J. Bielawa Collection.*

violence finally left him swinging at the end of a rope, Delaney, all alone, whispered of his New Haven birthright to the executioner.

Red-bearded and barrel-chested Cast Iron Bill would prove to be a madman hauled out of the tides of time. America's golden age of piracy had been buried at sea more than ten decades prior to Delaney's birth; if only he had been fortunate enough to stomp along New England docks 125 years earlier, he would have found himself in amicable blunderbuss-toting company. Our Connecticut shores were no stranger to the scourge of piracy. Captain Kidd sailed Long Island Sound during the conclusion of the seventeenth century and, according to legend, boldly strode the streets of harbor-side Milford. Kidd's treasure is rumored to be still secreted somewhere along the Nutmeg coast. Indeed, New England hosted some of the fiercest sea-raiders known to history. Thomas Quelch (hanged in 1704) and his surly crew guzzled Marblehead rum while psychopathic torturer Ned Low (vanished circa 1724) haled from Boston.

William E. Delaney's early family life in New Haven had a direct bearing on his piratical destiny. When Billy was four years old, his mother died. The sad event cemented a burden of abandonment and unfulfilled wanderlust in him. His distraught father moved with young

Ned Low of Boston was only one of many New England pirates, but he may have been the most brutal. His reputation as a psychopathic torturer was legendary. In a good mood, he once offered a captured captain the choice of a stout drink or a pistol ball. New Haven's own pirate, William Delaney, exhibited a similar dark humor. *Drawing from Charles Ellms,* The Pirates Own Book.

William to Ireland, where they stayed just ten months before relocating to new opportunities in Melbourne, Australia. When Bill turned eight, his father remarried. The relationship between little William and his uncaring stepmother soured by the day; around the age of thirteen, Bill gathered what money he could, purchased a pistol and knife and ran away. Kicking around the gold mines of Geelong and the Aussie docks, William eventually took a seamen's pay and headed as far from Australia, and his stepmother, as possible. Delaney returned to the only home he knew, New Haven. Using the Elm City as his base, Bill got a job as the cook aboard a brig (possibly the *Morning Light*) plying between New Haven and Demerara (located off the north coast of South America).

Not long afterward, a London voyage proffered Delaney the impulsive opportunity to go a-pirating. After fourteen days aboard the packet ship on which he was employed, Bill and some of the crew mutinied. Renegades battled those loyal to the captain for four straight days until the ringleaders were clapped in irons. Delaney's battle injuries were minor—he'd suffered only a broken lip and bruised eye socket—but the vessel became tattered as the remaining rebellious seamen refused their duties. Once in the Thames River, seventeen men jumped ship and headed for Liverpool. Delaney signed aboard a New York–bound ship and then made the four-month passage to Hong Kong. In the British Colony, he fell into a row with the first mate and bashed the man's head in with a belaying pin. Sailors frantically hoisted the ensign, raising it upside down for the international signal for distress. Once the police boat pulled alongside and security clambered aboard, a terrific struggle erupted, halted only when the outnumbered Delaney was subdued at the points of multiple cutlasses. After serving four grueling months on a chain gang, Bill hunkered down in front of a glowing wreck-wood fire; gazing across the beach, through the swirling embers, he resolved to turn pirate. Delaney christened himself Cast Iron Bill. Obsessed with the villainy of the "brethren of the coast," he took on a second alias as well, the Red Pirate. For a year or so, Cast Iron Bill survived as a Hong Kong river pirate.

While the American Civil War raged, Delaney served twelve months onboard a British man-of-war. The entire time, he schemed to capture the vessel and head for Caribbean waters to fight for the Confederacy. During his next adventure, while on a bark loaded with silks and teas heading for San Francisco, Delaney again made plans to kill the officers, capture the ship and, this time, sail for the Sandwich Islands. He was betrayed by a sailor who overheard the plot in the forecastle, and when Bill took his position at the wheel, he was knocked down and chained. Delaney was carted off to a California jail to await trial. For two months, he remained in a cell. Apparently nothing could stand in the way of Cast Iron Bill for long. He would later brag how he made his escape fettered to a thirty-two-pound ball.

Thinking it best to evade prison by hiding in plain sight, Delaney joined the ranks of the United States Army in California. The felon remained just long enough to receive one pay and then deserted with a few comrades (stealing the best horses in camp). Eventually, the small band made it as far as the Rouge River in Oregon, where they commandeered a twenty-ton schooner. Three hundred miles down the coast, the crew purposely scuttled the vessel. A crazed bunch, the men got into an argument and fell to knives and pistols; some, like Delaney, got out alive. It took a year working as a sealer for Bill to gain enough cash to make his way back to San Francisco, where he signed-on as a crewman for a voyage to Honolulu.

After sailing the Pacific, the ever-restless Delaney decided it was time to seek his family roots and ventured to Ireland; there he enjoyed a three-year stay with a few uncles. It became painfully obvious that he missed his father. Family convinced William, and paid his way, to rejoin his father in Melbourne. All was fine for only too briefly: his stepmother once again vehemently rejected Bill's presence. The deflated young man took his father's suggestion and went to work in the Geelong Mines as a stevedore. Delaney's never-back-down nature dictated another savage run-in, this time with the mining camp's intimidating bully. William Reid liked sharpening his bad reputation among the miners and townspeople as an unbeatable boxer. The Red Pirate whipped him in a rough and gouging slugfest. A rematch was arranged in which the winner would receive $800. The two fighters went at it for an incredible seventy rounds. Blood and pus rained down on the cheering vampiric miners. When the bell announced the start

Delaney's stories seem so outlandish as to be impossible. Yet the places, dates, ships and events he boasted of being personally a part of actually do check out when compared to historical facts. Cast Iron Bill related that he served on the gunboat *Unadilla* off the coast of China. This ship was part of the newly established Asiatic Squadron established during 1867–68. The following year, the *Unadilla* was sold and became the merchant *Dang Wee*. This lithograph, circa 1861, was issued with different ships' names to represent many, if not all, of the U.S. Navy's Unadilla-class gunboats. It was sunk in a collision off Hong Kong in 1870. *Courtesy of the U.S. Navy.*

of the seventy-first round, Delaney, crimped with three broken ribs, rose slowly from his stool. Reid, wailing with pain, could not counter; his right eye dangled loosely from its socket. The New Haven sailor and new hero of the miners stood alone, victorious in the center ring.

The Red Pirate could never remain landlocked. He shipped back to Hong Kong and deserted the schooner *Sunshine* to join the American gunboat *Unadilla*. Once aboard, he followed his preferred profession: combatant. The ship engaged Chinese pirates. Delaney was transferred to the U.S. naval ship *Maumee* and finished his enlistment on the frigate *Piscataqua*.

All the while, New England was calling. Homesick, Delaney wandered the streets of New Haven before the ocean's grip brought him to New Bedford. He signed aboard the whaler *Callao* as a boat-steerer and sailed around the Horn for the Pacific. Whaling life was both grueling and routine, the latter being the bane of Cast Iron Bill's existence. When the *Callao* reached Honolulu, he fled with nine other shipmates. The ship's owners did not take such matters lightly. Two days later, he was apprehended. For punishment, Delaney was secured in a wooden barrel where, for three weeks, he was fed through the small spigot hole bored into the side.

Within forty-eight hours of being restored to deck duty, the rebellious cask-dweller sighted land. From the corners of their eyes, Bill's toiling crewmates witnessed a strong-arm vault and a flash of red hair flinging over the ship's gunwale. The Red Pirate swam to shore. Sick of the rabble-rouser, the captain was surely relieved: "Maybe Delaney will drown, or better yet, his sour disposition might sweeten the table of cannibals." Cast Iron Bill had a hearty laugh while shaking himself dry; he donned a loincloth and resided with the island's native people for the next two months. Then, Billy talked his way aboard a sandalwood trader and sailed to Sydney; from Australia, he returned to New York aboard a cargo ship full of wool. There ended the deep sea adventures of the Red Pirate.

It was not an easy chore, but over the course of a decade, Bill had garnished a loathsome and toxic reputation on both sides of the Pacific. With such a robust and noticeable tear sheet, Delaney had little choice but to grab his ditty bag and enter the northeast Atlantic's coasting trade. While aboard a schooner, Cast Iron Bill tossed the first mate from the deck to the dock, breaking the man's collar bone and causing a warrant to be issued for his arrest. Previous experience illustrated that the military was a good situation to escape to, and the army deserter again joined up. This time, he signed with the marine corps. Stationed at first in the Brooklyn Naval Yard, Bill was transferred to Portsmouth, New Hampshire. Like clockwork, he got entangled with authority once more. Probably not the best person to stand guard over anything of value, Cast Iron Bill turned a blind eye (with an extended palm) during large-scale copper heists taking place on the base. His leatherneck career was quickly done. Awaiting court martial, Bill escaped. Later he boasted, "I stayed three weeks [as a marine], and one night swam the river Piscataqua, made my way to Boston, and then to Philadelphia [on a passing coal ship]." He would spend the next two and a half years working the coasting trade, transporting cargos to every dock along the northeast.

Atlantic ports from New Hampshire to Virginia waited to be plucked by the Red Pirate. He and a buddy robbed a southern oyster vessel in Hampton Roads; threw ill-gotten treasure at factory girls in Fall River, Massachusetts; and pounded whiskey and fought in fifty taverns across coastal New England. As mate aboard a Fall River schooner, Delaney fell from the mast, "eighty-two feet," roared Bill, and was hospitalized with hemorrhaging lungs. He "fought the cook [while plying out of Philadelphia] and thumped the life out of him" and was compelled to join the schooner *Clara Belle* running between Philly and Salem. Bill signed on as cook, but his knowledge of sailing got him promoted to first mate. Incapable of taking orders, he argued fiercely with the *Clara Belle*'s captain and departed the ship in Port Johnson, New Jersey. There, the Red Pirate was signed on as mate of the coasting schooner *Joseph E. Potts*; it would be Delaney's final voyage.

The *Joe Potts* haled from Port Jefferson, New York, under the command of sixty-two-year-old Captain Leven Lawrence. Laden with coal bound for Stonington, Connecticut, the schooner anchored a day out of Jersey off Long Island in Cow Bay (today known as Manhasset Bay) near King's Point. The following evening, Friday, August 27, 1875, while the ship waited on a favorable wind, teenage cook Augustus Tuthill summoned Delaney and the captain to dinner. Spontaneously, noise of a struggle compelled Tuthill and crew member Charles F. Harris to peek into a porthole.

In the galley, the pirate and captain were arguing over the food when Delaney knocked the old man to the floor. Delaney wrestled and then strangled the captain, while ramming a whittled block of wood into his mouth. The powerful bandit continued choking Lawrence with his bare hands. Rifling the cabin, the pirate discovered a pistol, and from inside a small satchel he grabbed two twenty-dollar bills and a five-cent piece. Delaney swigged out of a nearby whiskey bottle and choked Captain Lawrence a third time. He carried the body to a stateroom and secured the door with ropes. Heading up on deck, Cast Iron Bill leveled the weapon at the two crewmates and demanded that they row him to shore, ordering his captives to bring the dory

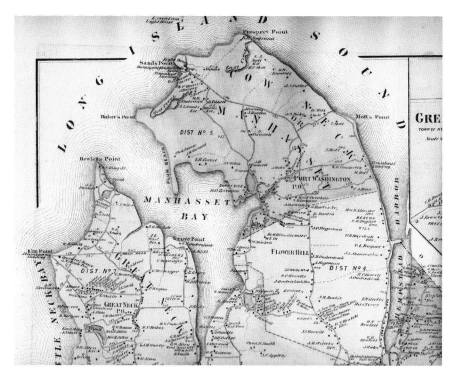

When the *Joseph E. Potts* put into Cow Bay, listed here as Manhasset Bay, to await a fair wind, sea robber Delaney made plans to plunder the captain and ship. It is remarkable to consider that Cast Iron Bill's worldwide piratical adventures brought him full circle back to the threshold of New Haven, located not too far distant across Long Island Sound from this cove. *Map from Frederick W. Beers's Atlas of Long Island, New York.*

in stern first so that Delaney did not have to walk past the young men when he disembarked. From Throg's Neck, he got to New York City and then took a train to Pennsylvania. Bill was apprehended not even a month later, located in a Philadelphia jail for a robbery he committed on the banks of the Delaware River. He'd pulled a four-day drinking binge, which probably lulled him into using his real name (and surely his birthplace too), at police headquarters, which led to his extradition.

Hauled back to New York, Delaney was placed in the Queens County jailhouse in North Hempstead. His furious temperament caused the jailers to chain Delaney to the floor. But the powerful pirate had other ideas. Near the end of September, through brute force, he eventually loosened the pins securing his chains to the ground and wrenched the heavy clasps of his cell door until they were just ready to be ripped loose. Delaney would have exploded to freedom except for the grinding metallic noises he had generated during his secretive work. The village blacksmith was summoned, and new chains were tightly placed around Delaney's ankles; the links were now bolted into the cell floor using eighteen-inch-long screws.

On October 20, the trial commenced. Officer James W. Smith of Flushing, who escorted Delaney from Pennsylvania back to New York, stated that the defendant confessed on the train to strangling Lawrence and, after taking a draught of whiskey, going back into the room and "[giving] the old man's throat another squeeze." Delaney steadfastly denied the conversation ever took place, reasoning that the lawmen fabricated the story to ensure part of the reward money. The next day, the defense attorney's assertion that Captain Lawrence died of heart failure fell short, and after a mere twenty-minute deliberation, the jury found the Red Pirate guilty of murder. Judge Armstrong declared, "Hear now the sentence of the court, that you be taken to the prison from whence you came, and thence on Friday, December 10th between the hours of ten and two o'clock, by the Sheriff of Queens County, to the place of execution, and there hanged by the neck until you are dead; and may God, who alone can forgive, have mercy upon you."

While incarcerated, Delaney's bravado quickly drained before his jailers' eyes. He started coughing up blood, apparently from recurring hemorrhaging lungs. He refused to eat; and in addition, the Quakers and social workers visiting to save his soul admitted Delaney was slipping into insanity. Concerned about the prisoner's health, William's attorney, George A. Mott, called on his client. The moment the guards were out of sight, Delaney lept from his cot and seized the lawyer by the shoulders. Repeatedly, the prisoner hissed, "Give me your knife." The attorney protested that he did not have a knife and blurted out, quite frightened, that a weapon would never get him out of his chains. Delaney energetically whispered close to the attorney's face, explaining that his insanity was mere trickery and that he had already filed through his shackles. The saw marks were disguised with bread crumbs and dust. Fearful for his life, attorney Mott pretended to go along with the escape plan. He promised to return to Delaney's cell with a large knife (under the pretext of telling the guards he'd forgotten to tell the prisoner something important). The pirate was "tremulous with joy," according to the November 18, 1875 *Long Island Times*, exuberantly whispering, "I'll never forget the act as long as I live." Delaney then shared his plot: shaking free of the chains, he'd fake knocking Mott to the ground, and when the guards raced into the cell, he'd slit his captors' throats.

Once Mott was safely outside the madman's cell, the shocked attorney informed the sheriff. The following day five guards were required to overpower the enraged Delaney. It was true; his shackles had been cut through and the slits camouflaged with crumbs, and even more surprising, a hole was discovered leading to an adjoining cell. Two other prisoners next door, not in chains, had conspired in the pirate's escape. Delaney's bedding concealed a sharpened metal spring that had been used as a saw. His illness, bleeding lungs, was faked, too. He'd been secretly cutting himself deep inside his nostrils and sucking in the blood, only to feign a wracking cough at the right moment. Cast Iron Bill was dragged to another cell and placed in a new set of irons. Amazingly, within a few days, he had again chiseled through these heavy chains and set about destroying his latest brick lodgings.

The day before his execution, Delaney seemed a man calm beyond concern. The Red Pirate had asked for a haircut and a shave that afternoon; the visiting barber whistled aloud that he'd never once seen a head or neck so huge. That evening, Delaney's arms were tied behind his back, and the shackles were humanely removed from his badly bruised ankles. New black pants were tugged onto his frame, whereupon he gazed down admiringly at their cut and commented just how good a fit they were. While Undersheriff Benjamin Rushmore officially pronounced the death warrant aloud, Delaney laughed uproariously, guffawing that it sounded "nice enough to be an invitation to a ball."

Cast Iron Bill took a cheerful notion about being allowed to stretch his legs with a jailhouse stroll. When his cell door swung open, he stepped into the corridor smiling, "I'll take a walk *now*; there's no knowing where I'll be walking tomorrow night." Police at the end of the corridor looked in through the bars at the bound prisoner and sympathetically inquired, "How do you feel, Bill?" "Like having a drink," he retorted, "have you got a bottle in your pocket?" At the other end of the hall, Delaney, so familiar with a ship's galley, peered into the jail's kitchen. "There's big Annie," the pirate jovially quipped, "she's got as much breadth of beam as a Dutch frigate." Escorted with a bevy of guards, he traversed cell to cell pausing a moment before each iron grate to bid the occupant a sad farewell.

Back in his own cell, Delaney shook his bowed head, mindfully explaining that he hadn't employed the captain's stolen pistol or a nearby hatchet because he hadn't meant "to kill the old bloke. All I wanted was his money." He ruefully asked about two other prisoners who'd been hanged a year ago and how brave they acted walking to the scaffold: "How'd they die? Were they afraid?" A keeper told him that they didn't flinch. "Well," the Red

Pirate straightened his shoulders, "they didn't die any braver than Delaney will die. You won't see me flinch."

A few days before his execution, Delaney requested pen and paper and wrote an exacting confession regarding the Cow Bay murder, as well as an erudite account of the adventures and many clamorous tidings he'd confronted in the course of his spare twenty-four years. He wrote that the two boys aboard the *Joseph E. Potts* were as guilty as he, in that Augustus Tuthill told Delaney where the captain had hid $140 and that they would split the money. He warned in his long letter that his four brothers, all over six feet tall and weighing more than two hundred pounds apiece (and "all of them more desperate" than he), would be coming to Queens County to make amends. At some point, he also composed a chantey reminiscent of old piratical verse. The prisoner signed his autobiographical tale:

> *Wm. E. Delaney, alias Red Pirate, alias Cast-Iron Bill, who fought 100 pitched battles and never was beat. If I had one friend, Hempstead Jail would not hold me five seconds. But I am far from friends, but my brothers know it.*

He closed the epistle:

> *Now for revenge.*

By surprising coincidence, another inmate in the Hempstead jail, serving thirty days for vagrancy, turned out to be a shipmate of Bill's (his name was reported as either Hamilton or Wickham). The old salt was brought into the condemned man's cell. The Red Pirate regaled his friend and captors with boisterous sea stories. Bill's supper arrived, consisting of a plate of large oysters, pickled cabbage, fresh-baked bread and butter, two bowls of coffee and two fresh crullers. He asked for more oysters, which were freely provided. The men about the room watched amazingly as Bill devoured enough food for two men. Joking with those in the cells around him, Bill answered a serious question that, yes, he was indeed married to a woman in Fall River. He sighed, wishing that she'd just have visited him at least once "with a couple of files and a concave saw hidden in a bun." At eleven o'clock, he asked for another meal and was supplied cold roast beef, bread, cheese and tea, which he ate with conspicuous delight. He requested and heartily puffed away on a cigar. At a little before two in the morning, he lay down, his arms tied behind his back, and quietly sang sailor songs to himself. He spoke with his guards, explaining he never meant to kill Captain Lawrence, just steal his money and ruminating that "if he knew what a fix he would be caught in, he would have finished the two boys [his crew members] as well as the captain." He sighed listlessly, stating again that he had handed the teenagers half the stolen money. At four o'clock, he fell asleep, and ever the pirate, he muttered, "Dead men tell no tales." Delaney napped for about two hours, awoke for a bit and turned over and fell into a deep sleep until 9:15 a.m. He had fried eggs and toast for breakfast and asked the priest if he would be kind enough to write to his father in Australia and his uncle in Ireland.

At 11:35 a.m., the sheriff and undersheriff led the procession to the jail yard gallows. Delaney strode next, flanked by two priests. He walked firmly and deliberately with his head held high. A long double line of policemen filed behind. To counter any escape efforts, a number of special officers had been sworn-in that day, in addition to twenty Brooklyn and Long Island City constables, who were stationed inside the jailhouse and outside the prison walls (among a large crowd where vendors sold clam chowder and hawked morbid souvenir photographs of Delaney) as well as within the enclosure surrounding the gallows. Without hesitation, the condemned man walked onto the platform and stared out across a twitching sea of upturned faces. A cold stiff wind, carrying salty brine, blew in from the Sound, most certainly bringing a wave of open-ocean memory to the young sailor. A far cry from the warm wreck-wood fire on the banks of the China Sea years ago where he vowed a life of piracy.

Delaney coughed, cleared his throat and addressed the crowd of three hundred at his feet. He warmly thanked Sheriff Charles Sammis, the lawman's wife and all his keepers; his last words were, "The crime I committed I never intended to commit. But I die repentant and ask forgiveness. I hope my soul will be received into heaven." He shook hands with the sheriff, the jailors and the two priests. A constable adjusted the bulging knot just below the condemned man's left ear. The black hood was placed atop his head and pulled down over his newly cut short red hair. The sheriff nodded to the hangman who cut the rope attached to a 312-pound weight, lifting Delaney in the air about three feet, but far too slowly. For about a minute, the pirate's hands convulsed. The rest of his body was unnaturally placid. He remained dangling for eighteen minutes. Like his victim, the Red Pirate, too, was strangled to death. Cast Iron Bill was buried in a five-dollar coffin.

After the hanging, Delaney's chest-pounding escapades were attacked by New York newspapers as being pure delusion. Editors stained their columns ballyhooing that the farcical pirate's tales were far too incredible to accept as even remote possibility. They reported that as he walked to the noose, some in the crowd jeered because the public had branded Delaney a savage fool and a liar.

However, scouring nineteenth-century sources only recently made available, a handful of tattered government documents go a long way to bolster the Red Pirate's swaggering tales. While chained to the floor of that Long Island jailhouse, Delaney confessed to many crimes and reiterated serving time in various prisons, all of which he was able to escape from (except for the last one). A single sentence discovered in the *United States Army's Register of Enlistments* supports Delaney's outlandish exploits: a sailor by the name of William E. Delany, enlisted in the Twelfth Infantry while in San Francisco. The private deserted May 28, 1871. It was duly noted that the wanted man had red hair and was born in New Haven. A year later, on August 19, 1872, military records show Delaney enlisting in the marines. The incorrigible soldier was imprisoned for an unspecified crime just three weeks later. In late October 1872, he deserted once again.

Three years later, near the New Haven home that meant so much to William Delaney, the wicked path and biting pen of New England's last pirate came to an abrupt end.

———— ·❖· ————

For the first time since 1875, pirate Delaney's final verse, complete and unabridged, is here reprinted:

*My Dying Rhyme.*

*I.*
*Come all you kind young men,*
*Around me draw nigh;*
*And I will sing you a song,*
*That will draw tears to your eye.*
*My name is Delaney, that I'll never deny.*
*I am an innocent man and condemned to die.*

*II.*
*My mother died when I was but a child;*

*My father he raised me, although I was wild;*
*My father got married, but he dearly loved me,*
*But with a stepmother I could not agree.*

III.

*I left my dear father*
*At the age of thirteen, and went a seafaring*
*To plough the salt seas;*
*But I'm now in a dungeon with a broken heart,*
*Waiting for the sad day when my soul must depart.*

IV.

*I hired with a captain,*
*And as mate I did go,*
*The death of that captain I think you all know;*
*For to get his money*
*I tried all my skill,*
*With intention to rob,*
*But not for to kill.*

V.

*It was Officer Smith who swore my life away,*
*But my curse is upon him, by night and by day.*
*I had a packed jury.*
*And I not worth a cent,*
*For to find me guilty they were fully bent.*

VI.

*My trial is over, my sentence is passed,*
*A verdict of guilty my jury found fast;*
*On the tenth of December my life will depart,*
*Which will leave my aged father,*
*With a broken heart.*

VII.

*I fear not the gallows,*
*Or I fear not to die;*
*When my soul on to Heaven*
*With the angels will fly.*

*And when on the gallows*
*These words I will say,*
*Good people around me*
*For my poor soul pray.*

The chantey was inscribed:

*Written by William Delaney, who was not afraid to face no man, big or little; the hero of 4 prize fights; the shortest fight ever I fought was 62 rounds out of 500 men on board of a man of war. I could make any of them take water.*

*Delaney, alias Red Pirate, alias cast iron Bill.*

## Chapter 7

# Trapped in a Lighthouse with a Madman

*Insane impulses, he knew, were like the waves of the sea about him. They
writhed and twisted and arose too high, and then burst into the foam of madness.*
*"Madhouse Light"*
*Charles Francis Coe, 1929*

*The talk always came back to Lights: Lights of the Channel; Lights on forgotten
islands, and men forgotten on them.*
*"The Disturber of Traffic"*
*Rudyard Kipling, 1891*

Sullen on its rocky outcropping at the mouth of New Haven Harbor, the
Southwest Ledge Lighthouse might as well have been built on the dark
side of the moon, yet somehow it looms tauntingly within reach. Like a cursed
diamond glinting in a museum's display case, it elicits a peculiar fascination.
From the elevated portion of the thruway, commuters by the thousands
glimpse the lighthouse every day; but except for periodic maintenance visits
to tend the foghorn and flashing red beacon, no one enters this light tower.
Empty rooms are abandoned to time. Stillness floods this cast-iron structure
like a storm surge. Only the dust on the steps leading up to the lantern room
seems to shift with ghostly boot prints of madness.

The tower's first beam of light slit Long Island Sound's darkness New
Year's Day 1877. Over the decades, a number of thankful sailors came to
owe their lives to the Southwest Ledge Lighthouse. During the time it was

Southwest Ledge Lighthouse. Dedicated on January 1, 1877, this beacon and foghorn saved numerous lives. The breakwater stretching east from the lighthouse to Quixes Ledge was constructed between April 22, 1880, and February 22, 1890. *Courtesy of the United States Coast Guard.*

manned by a keeper and his assistant, the dire pendulum of monotony and storm made this stony perch a stern and godless place just a handful of miles from bustling downtown.[14]

The lighthouse design was a unique conglomeration of shapes. The eight-sided, cast-iron building rested on a cylindrical foundation and rose forty-five feet. The spacious cellar, encased by boulders, was dug beneath the waterline. Dual cisterns, which collected the roof's rainwater for drinking and washing, were placed here. Eight tons of coal, groceries and sundry other supplies were stowed in the cellar as well. A stairway to the first floor led up to a parlor, sitting room and kitchen; the next level held two bedrooms. The last flight of steps led to the watch room, where fuel and light-related supplies were stored. The top floor, accessed by a ladder in the center of the room, brought the two workers to the glass enclosure that housed the revolving lantern. Men stationed there entered the lighthouse from their boats by climbing a twenty-five-rung ladder to a narrow balcony that led to the hatch that opened onto the main floor. When seas proved too dangerous, keepers kept in touch with the mainland by using a system of flags (replies were hoisted from Five Mile Light on the point).

From its inception, the quarters were far too cramped. Dampness, mold and roach infestation were constant battles for the inmates. A serious problem developed with the cisterns turning the drinking water rancid. It seemed that the heartless site harbored something foreboding. At one point, the entire tower was painted a glaring, prophetic red, symbolically, the color associated with blinding anger, madness or evil. No one could have guessed the hue swathed over this lonely structure was as much a warning about the dangerous ledge lurking just below the water's surface as it was about the sentiments churning within a man's consciousness.

Prior to his arrival in New Haven, Nils Nilson (sometimes spelled Nelson) was the assistant keeper stationed at Sakonnet Light in Rhode Island. On July 23, 1903, heavy seas swamped and dashed a mail boat on the rocks near that light. The sailor aboard, George Child, managed to wedge himself into the crevices of a ledge, clinging there for half an hour before Nilson placed his own life at risk and rescued the doomed man. Just shy of a year after Nilson's gallantry, the burly man was recognized with a congressional gold lifesaving medal. Nils was named Sakonnet's head keeper, but in 1907, he was

This rare photograph of Jorgen Tonnesen shows the distinguished head keeper of Southwest Ledge Lighthouse about the time he barricaded himself in the upper reaches of the cast-iron tower. Born in 1843, the Norwegian was assistant keeper of the light from 1898 to 1905 and then became head keep in 1905. Despite being trapped with a deranged man, Tonnesen still maintained the light. He died in 1914 and was buried in East Lawn Cemetery, East Haven. *Courtesy of the Connecticut State Library.*

demoted for some unrecorded reason and transferred to the Southwest Ledge breakwater. The depressing and unhealthy conditions at the New Haven light ultimately contributed to tragedy. It was about November 1907 when keeper Jorgen Tonnesen noticed a perceptible difference in the temperament of his assistant.

At the time, some said it was the loneliness of Southwest Ledge (and modern-day pathologists might blame mind-altering molds or tainted water), but Nilson's temperament dated back to his earlier post in Rhode Island. Stationed at Southwest Ledge, his mental anguish completely ensnared him. On one particularly bleak autumn night, when the waves smacked barbed lips against the lighthouse foundation, assistant keeper Nilson went berserk. A

*Left*: Nils Nilson, the hero of Sakonnet Point Light in Rhode Island. Head keeper Nilson was awarded the gold lifesaving medal by the United States Coast Guard. Later, he was demoted and sent to the Southwest Ledge. Some blame the awful living conditions at the lonely New Haven lighthouse for his madness. *Courtesy Lighthouse Digest.*

*Below*: This architectural rendition illustrates the various levels and cramped rooms of the Southwest Ledge Lighthouse shared by the head keeper and his assistant. Jorgen Tonnesen barricaded himself in the oil room in an attempt to avoid his deranged ax-wielding mate. *Courtesy of the United States Coast Guard.*

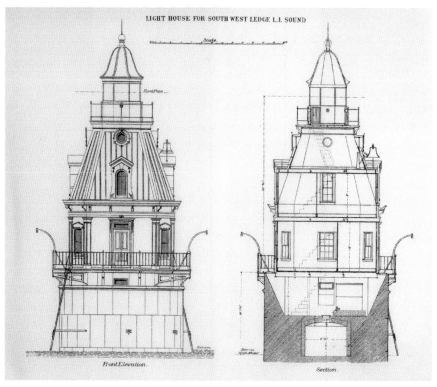

trifling disagreement between the keepers set Nils storming off in search of a weapon. Imitating Stephen King's future ax-wielding demon Jack Torrance in *The Shining*, Nils terrorized keeper Tonnesen, chasing him through the lighthouse. Jorgen could never abandon his lifesaving post, so in order to remain on the rock, he barricaded himself in the oil room just below the lantern (which allowed him access to fuel and the light). Nilson surrendered chopping at the hatch and exited the tower. Lowering the keeper's small boat, he rowed to New Haven.

Alone with his thoughts and pounding heart, Tonnesen realized his dangerous situation. On any given night, isolated in the lighthouse, a madman could sneak into his bedroom and slit his throat. The head keeper decided not to report the attack. Instead, he summoned his brother-in-law Bernt Thorstensen to remain on the breakwater as a watchman. Following an extended peaceful interlude, Nilson, a few weeks later, once more grabbed the keeper, pinning him against the bulkhead. Bernt pulled the lunatic off his brother-in-law, but only after Nilson whispered that he'd slash the keeper's throat with a butcher knife.

On Friday, January 17, 1908, Nilson headed for the mainland to retrieve supplies. He didn't return to the light for three days. Reluctantly back on Southwest Ledge on Tuesday, January 21, the deranged man flew into a fit and sawed away at his own throat with a carving knife. Hearing the commotion, Bernt Thorstensen overpowered Nils. That same day, the poor fellow again placed a blade to his throat and, for a second time, was breathlessly subdued. Bernt pitied the man, making him promise to visit a mainland doctor. Much calmer, Nils lowered the small sailboat and headed for the city.

In an obvious cry for help, Nilson marched from the dock to visit Reverend John O. Bergh, the overseer of the Seamen's Bethel and Home. Located at 61 Water Street, the chapel and living quarters provided a safe retreat for seafarers. The assistant keeper requested a knife to cut his throat. Reverend Bergh comforted the man and immediately sought professional help for Nils. But without a crime being committed, the reverend was frustratingly informed, neither the police nor John V. Rattlesdorfer (the superintendant of Charities and Corrections) could lift a numbed bureaucratic finger. At the time, the local hospitals also refused to admit insane persons. Patrolmen did arrive at the waterfront church, but Nils was not taken into custody. Bernt Thorstensen, still concerned for Nils, rowed to town after he was relieved by his brother-in-law and searched for the beleaguered assistant keeper. That night, with no one to rescue the confused lifesaver, Nilson walked down to the docks at the foot of Hamilton Street, not very far from the Seamen's Bethel, and cut his throat. Fifty-nine-year-old oyster-police captain David W. Risley found the body.[15] Nils Nilson succeeded in his bloody goal.

The harbor was far too rough to make a safe voyage out to the light. At sunrise, Tonnesen was informed by flags waving atop the old Five Mile Light, "Come to shore, there is a problem." When the Sound relaxed, he rowed to town, where he arranged the funeral.

Reverend Bergh conducted services at Lewis & Maycock's mortuary chapel. Four seamen from the bethel acted as pallbearers. The casket closed over Nils wearing his gold medal. According to the *New Haven Evening Register*, Nilson was interred at Evergreen Cemetery. No record of a grave marker exists; perhaps a lack of funds or the sad nature of his demise precluded a gravestone. Thus, there is no precise spot to visit and pay deserved respects to this tragic hero, except when one looks out at lonely Southwest Ledge Light. There, at the breakwater's end is the truly sacred site, where Nils Nilson wrestled with his mind-born demons and struggled to serve the sea and the revolving beacon still searches for its lost assistant keeper.

*Chapter 8*

# The Czar's Guard and the Acid Queen

*My work is done, now look at him*
*He's never been more alive*
*His head it shakes, his fingers clutch*
*Watch his body writhe*

*The Who*
*Pete Townshend, 1969*

Frank Sokolowsky's face was melting. The sudden onslaught of crushing throat and stomach pain propelled the tall, and up to a few moments ago, strikingly handsome man from bed. Disoriented, his blue lips chomped feverishly for air as he crashed through the first-floor flat and onto the front porch. The soft murmur of crickets abruptly ceased. It was three in the morning on Saturday, June 26, 1920. Along New Haven's refined Beers Street, alarmed neighbors peered through lace curtains toward the bone jarring shrieks. Frank was able to shout a few raspy words before collapsing, "Police! Doctor! Help!" Half a block away, attendants at Grace Hospital heard the commotion and dispatched an ambulance. Too late, though, Sokolowsky lay dead, his face and head drenched and still hissing with sweet-smelling carbolic acid.

Whatever took place inside 25 Beers Street could probably be answered by Frank's wife, Alexandra. But Mrs. Sokolowsky was conspicuously missing. Standing in her nightgown while a doctor examined the dead man, she

Frank Sokolowsky. Versed in eight languages, educated in prerevolutionary Russia and a charismatic labor leader in booming Connecticut brass mills, this debonair New Haven immigrant may have carried some of the twentieth century's greatest secrets. *Courtesy of the Connecticut State Library.*

was suddenly swallowed by the Beers Street night. Detectives surveying the scene didn't need to stretch cognitive reasoning very far to nod in agreement that this was surely a case of extreme domestic violence.

The couple and their five-year-old daughter, Aldona, had just moved to New Haven in early June. In that short span of three weeks, the landlord, who lived upstairs, saw the Sokolowsky's as a blissful couple; other neighbors, however, complained that they'd heard an intense argument just two hours before the Polish (some said Lithuanian) immigrant fell dead. Police officers and the medical staff shook their heads, "What a terrible way to go." Maybe Sokolowsky committed suicide. Why else, they wondered, would one swallow such a large dose of acid?

Then the whispers began.

It was said Sokolowsky was born in Russia, where he graduated from an upper-echelon university. Another rumor stated Sokolowsky was an accomplished artist from Toronto. It was also attested Sokolowsky was a Boston sewing machine salesman. The dapper Sokolowsky was fluent in eight languages. Still, he'd related to friends how he owned a shoe store in Brooklyn. Frank threw lavish parties, ate at the best restaurants and, once, upon meeting a beautiful woman on a New York street, charmed her with a fifteen-dollar flower bouquet (more than a week's pay for many factory workers during that era). Suddenly, the chameleon Frank Sokolowsky, if indeed that was his real name, shunted into an enigma who may have provoked or, in some manner, proved meddlesome to any number of individuals, organizations or, as detectives would soon discover, certain foreign heads of state.

## WHO'S WHO AMONG WORLD AGITATORS

The authorities and Sokolowsky's extensive array of former associates burned to find out this man's true identity. Police departments in Bridgeport, Waterbury and New Haven as well as up and down the factory-roaring Naugatuck Valley recognized Sokolowsky as a labor organizer. Newspapers of the day preferred splashing him with yellow ink and applying the Red epithet of "agitator." Dating back a year earlier, to 1919, Sokolowsky had been an important and charismatic speaker in Waterbury and Ansonia brass mills. These factories were a vital component of America's industrial strength. Their massive, city-engulfing plants produced so much of the ubiquitous metal that Waterbury was dubbed the Brass Capital of the World. (It was only the pervasive use of plastic during the 1970s that dethroned the alloy.) After the First World War, demand for the metal was in flux, and workers insisted on a shorter workweek (from fifty-five to forty-four hours) as well as higher pay (more than fifty-five cents an hour). During April 1920, Sokolowsky, as a member of the American Federation of Labor, became an energetic spokesperson prompting unskilled, non-English speaking Russian, Polish, Lithuanian and Italian laborers to walk off the job. Soon, they were joined by skilled workers. Waterbury streets surged with over fifteen thousand men and women marching on the brass mills. The city sat on a volatile powder keg with the American Federation of Labor (AFL) in a power struggle with the New England Workers Association (NEWA). Management had snipers placed on the roofs of their vast brick fortresses. A bomb was detonated by a rogue anarchist. Sweating eyeball to eyelash confrontations between police and strikers led to riot and, inevitably, to bloodshed.

Throughout the months of tumult, Sokolowsky gave humane voice to incarcerated workers, informing the public that when "strikers were arrested they were locked up eight men in a cell, unable to sit down or [lie] down, and compelled to stay [in the lock-up] all night without food." He advocated a conservative and peaceful approach to dealing with the moneyed owners. Radicals among the strikers railed at what they deemed Sokolowsky's caving-in. The two warring unions joined forces and took their directives from the nationally powerful AFL. Sokolowsky surely generated boundless jealousy with his newfound sway over local leader Ira M. Ornburn. The linguist's voice of pacifism got him branded by fellow workers, in the parlance of the recent war years, as a "defeatist," actively spurning the workers best interests. The *New York Times* noted three days before his death that Sokolowsky had addressed a large number of strikers in Waterbury, and it was obvious from his declarations that the organizer "had lost heart in the cause." Grumbling workers at the meeting shouted their displeasure. Worse, some felt that Sokolowsky's grand lifestyle was funded by factory owners and that the well-dressed intellectual had turned informant. Narrowing eyes and furrowed brows in brass-gilded overalls were calling him a double-crossing management spy. But the story became even more surreal.

## THE LADY IN RED IS A RED

All the while, the search for Mrs. Sokolowsky was widening. Investigators wondered how a mother could abandon her small child. They began to suspect that Alexandra may have witnessed her husband's slaying and was abducted or that the union leader's enemies had somehow enlisted Alexandra as a participant. The suspect had been traced as far as a fifteen-dollar taxi ride to Bridgeport. There, in the city's east side, she hid briefly among the Russian population before proceeding on to New York. At Grand Central Terminal, something telling may have occurred. Alexandra mailed a letter with a Grand Central postmark to 25 Beers Street. Supposedly, it was written by another woman; however, the ruse failed, as the envelope was addressed in Mrs. Sokolowsky's own hand. The question then arose if Alexandra was attracting blame for the murder to a person New Haven police were calling "the Wizard Woman."

After fleeing north into Canada, Alexandra then backtracked home to New Haven. In July, she rented a furnished York Street apartment for ten days, often walking in front of the Beers Street flat, hoping to catch a glimpse of her daughter Aldona (who was under the care of her former landlord and his wife, Mr. and Mrs. Walter Kelley). Police felt that Mrs. Sokolowsky was strategizing to kidnap the five-year-old. The abduction plot became clearer when Mrs. Sokolowsky was arrested in New York City on the night of August 1, 1920. For the previous week, Alexandra had been working in Harlem, on 122$^{nd}$ Street, as a domestic servant. During this time, she had sewn a young boy's blue suit as a disguise for her daughter. A black veil, a new hat and tortoise rim glasses were also among Alexandra's possessions and would be employed as a disguise of her own. The plan never went into effect. Detectives standing on 125$^{th}$ Street and Eighth Avenue spotted the fugitive; photographs had been circulated throughout the region featuring the petite,

Alexandra Sokolowsky and daughter Aldona. Mrs. Sokolowsky was sought by police across New England and Canada. Authorities wished to question her about possible involvement in the brutal acid attack on her husband. *Courtesy of the Connecticut State Library.*

110-pound, raven-haired, blue-eyed beauty. Perhaps subconsciously wishing to be apprehended, it was Alexandra's vibrant red blouse that garnered attention. Later, she explained that she'd always expected to be arrested in that glorious red outfit announcing her allegiance "as a Bolshevik."

# MAKE WAY FOR NICHOLAS II, EMPEROR OF ALL THE RUSSIAS

Czar Nicholas II. While investigating the Frank Sokolowsky affair, major American newspapers uncovered a mysterious connections between the Russian ruler, the New Haven man and some the world's most powerful leaders. *Courtesy of the Michael J. Bielawa Collection.*

When Alexandra was interrogated in the New York detention center known as the Tombs, those gathered around the table were shocked by what she shared. Supposedly, Sokolowsky was connected to one of the most powerful individuals on the planet: Czar Nicholas II. In Russia, Sokolowsky was known as Orloff or Orlorffski. The New Haven labor leader had once been a member of the Czar's Black 100, the ultra-nationalist Russian organization; even more startling, he had served as part of the Russian leader's personal bodyguard before the revolution and the royal family's murder at the hands of the Bolsheviks. It was also indicated that Sokolowsky might have worked with the brutal St. Petersburg secret police as well as the revolutionary assassin Yevno Azef (who later turned out to be a double agent for both the Socialist Revolutionary Party and the government). The czar had entrusted Orloff/Sokolowsky with delicate secret missions across Europe. While in London, some believed Orloff, in an effort to perpetuate the British monarchy, personally thwarted a plot against King George V, who was a cousin of the czar. At the outbreak of World War I, Sokolowsky departed the Continent to work as a spy for the Canadian government. Using the alias of Frank Genutis, the mysterious Russian crossed between Canada and the United States several times between 1914 and 1919. (A search of the Sokolowsky's Beers Street apartment revealed a passport in the name of Frank Genutis. Yet the photograph was undoubtedly that of the deceased labor leader.)

Orloff/Genutis, now called Sokolowsky, married Alexandra in Boston during 1914. At the time of their wedding, according to the August 15, 1920 *Hartford Courant*, they worked together as spies "under the auspices of the Russian Immigration Bureau." Alexandra, some postulated, was an anarchist double agent.

## THE ACT OF CONTRITION: WAS IT AN ACT?

Prior to her extradition to Connecticut, Alexandra Sokolowsky made a full and willing confession. On Friday, June 25, 1920, her husband had driven from their Beers Street home for labor meetings in Waterbury and then in Bridgeport. Alexandra had demonstrative doubts about her husband's whereabouts. He returned home very late that night, yet again. Over the course of the past half a month, she had found two letters in his pockets written in what looked like a feminine hand. Unable to read English, Alexandra asked a friend to translate what she deemed love notes. They'd been penned by twenty-six-year-old Brooklyn widow, Katherine, or Minnie, Neveloff. There seemed to have been a long bitter feud festering in the Sokolowsky household. A fellow Toronto artist friend of Frank's came forth after the murder and explained that the couple owned a rooming house in Canada; a year or so previous, they'd taken in an Italian American army deserter from Buffalo. Alexandra had fallen in love with the man. Mr. Sokolowsky departed for America, where he became involved in a friendship with another woman. After her Toronto affair, Alexandra sought reconciliation and followed her husband to New York City, where, quite by accident—like all true love stories—they serendipitously bumped into each other on a busy avenue. Mutual adoration for their daughter, Aldona, brought them back together. But Alexandra harbored the rage of the green-eyed monster. The letters she found in Frank's overcoat proved that her attractive husband was far too popular among American woman. A little acid, she thought, just enough to disfigure his face, would compel no one but her to love Frank Sokolowsky.

During her confession, Alexandra repeatedly told police that she never meant to kill her husband. Mrs. Sokolowsky stated, however, that she'd planned to disfigure Frank on more than one occasion, until finally, on June 26, 1920:

[Frank] *got home at 1:30 in the morning…He was very cross and told me to stay away from him. He went to bed, and at about 3 o'clock in the morning, while he was sleeping soundly, I got the bottle of carbolic acid, poured the poison into a glass and tossed it into his face. But I didn't mean to kill him.*

Alexandra continued:

[Neveloff] *is much prettier than I am. She was in love with my husband, and he planned to desert me for her. I didn't intend to kill him. I merely wanted to disfigure him and make him so hideous that neither Mrs. Neveloff nor any other woman would want him.*

The governors of New York and Connecticut signed documents allowing the return of the suspected murderer to New Haven. As the trial approached, insiders scratched their heads over the involvement of prominent Russian expatriates supporting Alexandra. The Reverend John Henry Bell, pastor of the Church of All Nations, which was at the epicenter of Russian activity in New York City, hired prominent local attorney Jacob P. Goodhart as Alexandra's defense. During the hearing, coroner Eli Mix testified that Frank A. Sokolowsky's death was due to carbolic acid poisoning and shock. Again Mrs. Sokolowsky explained that she never meant to kill her husband; her throwing the acid occurred during a jealous build-up and emotional explosion. On October 29, 1920, Judge Isaac Wolfe found the defendant guilty of manslaughter and sentenced Alexandra Sokolowsky to seven to ten years in the Wethersfield State Prison.

Although the case certainly appeared resolved, to this day there still remain a number of interesting and unanswered questions. How true are Sokolowsky's bizarre intrigues? Was there a cover-up? Some newspapers and police officers felt that Alexandra Sokolowsky took the fall for someone else. As for the main evidence of the love letters, widow Neveloff testified that she was merely good friends with Sokolowsky and that her notes were harmless, nothing could be misconstrued from their contents.

Was the slain labor leader protecting aristocratic pro-Russian interests in America that annoyed the Bolsheviks? The power plant at the Scoville brass mill had been built with the czar's own money. Or, in turn, were supporters of the deposed czarist regime seeking revenge because Sokolowsky was now on the side of the working class? Some American journalists felt that Communist influence within the Industrial Workers of the World, or the Wobblies, had a decisive hand in the Brass power struggle and Orloff/Sokolowsky's murder. Supposedly, while serving as a Canadian secret agent, Sokolowsky had frustrated the IWW's 1918 terrorist plans aimed at Toronto. When examining the mysterious life and violent death of Orloff—or Genutis or Sokolowsky—there isn't one but actually numerous webs of conspiracy dangling over the Beers Street neighborhood of a dapper Elm City super spy.

## Chapter 9

# Some Occurrences Regarding the Stolen Dead

*And the moon gazed on my midnight labours…who shall conceive the horrors of my secret toil, as I dabbled among the unhallowed damps of the grave.*
Frankenstein
*Mary Shelley, 1818*

*I have made candles of infants fat*
*The Sextons have been my slaves,*
*I have bottled babes unborn, and dried*
*Hearts and livers from rifled graves.*

*And my Prentices now will surely come*
*And carve me bone from bone,*
*And I who have rifled the dead man's grave*
*Shall never have rest in my own.*
*"Surgeon's Warning"*
*Robert Southey, 1799*

*"Father," said Young Jerry, as they walked along…*
*"What's a Resurrection-Man?"*
A Tale of Two Cities
*Charles Dickens, 1859*

December 29th, 1823
Dear Justin—

There is so much to write of which is taking place here in our quiet village of West Haven, Connecticut. Or rather, excuse my error, I should say "Orange." After all this time, it is not easy for your old uncle to adapt to our town's proud new title—a year since West Haven and North Milford combined and changed the name. Still, the village itself is not much altered, that is, the homesteads, churches and farms are surely identical. But the occupants of these abodes, the people you once knew…the citizens, dear Justin, are in a sort of inexplicable bind. Something is amiss, and I am, sadly, at a loss to offer any answer. What goads the townsfolk? I can not ascertain. However, one sad reality concerns Bathsheba Smith. Poor, poor Bathsheba. You remember the young thing. So pretty. She lived on her father, Laban's, farm just a couple miles west of the Green, out near Durand's place. Yes, yes I did write "lived." The consumption unjustly took her this very day. Just a sprite-full nineteen years of age. It's quite a tragedy, Justin. But mark my words nephew. As of now, I will compose a letter to share my observations each time I see or hear or feel whatever this thing is that affects our village. I hope to write of lighter matters. Yet I sense that something quite markedly odd is in the offing and will be proffered in ensuing ink.

Yr. affectionate UNCLE,
Mathus

Thursday, January 1st, 1824
Justin—

I so wish that I could share uplifting news this First day of '24. But the Cheer of the Season ceased as church bells announced the new-year. Instead, an audible Gasp filled our little Village. Bathsheba was committed to the earth today. Justin, you would be touched by the numbers of our dear friends, acquaintances and neighbors in attendance at the graveside service. So many gathered in the old Episcopal cemetery. Yes, nephew, the same graveyard we scurried passed on Autumn eves so long ago (as fast as our stout legs could fly!). Those moldy death-heads yet grimace atop forgotten mounds. And today, mourners gazed listlessly at the thawing ground as We each bowed heavy heads. "Poor, poor, Bathsheba," commented one fellow holding his top hat nex' me. "The young thing, so ill for so long…and to pass during Christmas-time." Someone replied, I marked not whom, "True. But oh, so radiant. She shares her beauty with the Angles!" I observed as the cluster of black-clad mourners moved closer toward the open grave, they seemed as tho they Willed, as One, to peer into the coffin and witness a last delightful glimpse of Bathsheba's exquisiteness. But it was nigh impossible. Already the heavy stone slab had been placed upon the head of the wooden box. The sexton cast handfuls of straw down upon the coffin. This practice (hushed voices explained to those feign of heart) was a method to dull the sorrowful thud of earth landing on the wooden lid. Men-folk, however, understood that the bundles of straw would slow the work of Resurrectionists. Any delay allows for the possibility of a citizen to overhear or stumble upon the grave-robbers struggling to accomplish their wicked Art. Naturally, in the days following a funeral, even a single wisp of straw scattered about the gravesite would offer a telltale clue that the burial had been desecrated.

With compassion and sadness being our mortar and stone, we squeezed tightly within our churchyard ring. Not for warmth mind you. And this, this is another odd matter, Justin. All along the Connecticut coast hereabouts, the weather, of late, has been strangely Warm, as if it were April and we collecting blossoms for your Mother. Ships' crews down at the chandlery tell me that as far-away as Albany and as far east as the Vin'yard they see no snow. And that being said, I can state that as far up the Connecticut River as Hartford, there is not a single sheet of ice. Don't think anyone here in West Haven, that is, I mean, Orange, is complaining, but this January's warmth is certainly peculiar. I am sorry; I meant to mention the mourners, so many of whom are friends. We were especially touched, in sympathetic manner, by the tears of one particular fellow. He has been a guest of Rev. Stebbins, marking the New Year with the good reverend's family. His face is a new one to our precious community—a student of medicine over in New Haven, I believe, or in some-way associated with Yale school. His name is Ephraim. Ephraim Colburn. Well, I must admit, watching the doleful cemetery assemblage, I noted his eyes certainly were red as coals burn-ing with the tears he shed for poor Bathsheba.

Yr. affectionate UNCLE,
Mathus

Sunday, January 4th, 1824
Dear Justin—

Events here in West Haven have caused me restless nights. The unseasonable, and thus jarring, warm temps. prompt me to entice sleep with late night jaunts. As I passed by the old PLATT Home during the wee hours of the 3rd, the clouds above opened and there, arching high within the constellation of Hercules, I did witness the glaring tail of a COMET. Perhaps OUR present days of science demand a reasoning mind, but I still shuddered on this lonely road, wondering, like our Puritan forbearers, at the thought of this celestial vision's evil portent. Vilely, my ponderings were too soon answered. As I drew nigh upon the dirt lane leading to Laban Smith's farm, I discerned the shrieks of a woman whom I immediately thought to be Mrs. Smith. Racing down the narrow dirt road and leaping upon the porch, I pounded incessantly on the farmhouse door. Slowly the entrance opened, and I was greeted by our trusted friend Laban, whose wild visage rendered him hardly recognizable. With no regard to his disheveled appearance, Smith eagerly bade me in. This I suddenly feared. He wished human comfort, I felt, due

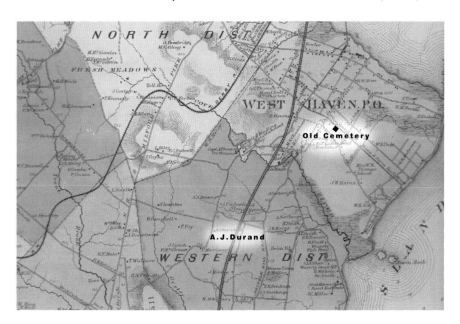

Roadmap to New England Horror. This map illustrates the downtown West Haven cemetery from which the body of nineteen-year-old Bathsheba Smith was buried and subsequently stolen. The Smith family farm was located in the area near A.J. Durand's home. *From Frederick W. Beers, Atlas of New Haven County.*

to a presence of inhuman confrontation. My emotions proved true. Mad-eyed Laban collapsed in a chair, sighing as he explained his sad eventides. Ever since young Bathsheba's burial, his wife had been assaulted by demon-borne dreams. He explained that Mrs. Smith, far too weak to join us in the living room, was each night awakened by a horrifying vision. Laban's beloved would rise from her pillow, he stated, screaming furiously that their daughter's body was not at peace, that her grave was molested by ghouls. Do pardon me, my young nephew, but I must break from this epistle. What will follow I FEEL is far too demonic…

Asking for Yr. Prayers,
Mathus

Tuesday, January 6th, 1824
Dear Justin—

I write to you this Twelfth Night with no merriment. Everyone in town is now keenly aware of Mrs. Smith's consistent and disquieting Nightmares. It was Laban's decision to deal with these hellish visions that led to her dreams being made public. Justin, it is a most pitiful sight to witness Mr. Smith. He is haggard and unkempt with the duty undertaken. Each night, until dawn, he guards Bathsheba's tomb. His only company is a shotgun, which he maintains loaded and at the ready to send any ghoul to its doom. It is not, my nephew, a rare event for graves to be pilfered. But by whom, you may inquire? Our medical colleges here in New England usually run from early November until February, Yale's medical lectures begin a tad earlier, in October, and commence for just four months, ending in January (thus lowering students' heating costs).[16] Lacking any facility for preservation, these months mark the Harvest-time for the Dead. Cadavers are acquired for dissection purposes. Physicians, who act as preceptors, and university Profs. need a fresh supply of bodies for study. An abhorrent practice that should be reserved solely for executed murderers, as in England (due to their Murder Act of 1752). But no Decree can outlaw Nightmare. Laban Smith is out there even now, alone, in this unseasonably warm fog, amid the death-heads and winged hourglasses. Waiting.

Yr. UNCLE,
Mathus

Sunday, January 11<sup>th</sup>, 1824

J——

I jot these lines in maddening haste. It is late at night, but before memory abandons a single detail, I must inform you, nephew, of what has transpired at the Old Cemetery. Oh, how I wish we could all be deafened to such gruesome news.

Bathsheba is missing! Laban Smith had willfully ceased standing guardian over his poor Daughter's grave. Mrs. Smith felt that time enough had intervened, that the body would be in a state of decay rendering the pretty girl unsatisfactory for anatomic examination. Yet to be safe, as is common cemetery practice, Smith arranged stones and pebbles on the grave so that should they be disturbed, the Family would be alerted to a grave robbery. This d——d warm weather. If only there had been a ground cover of snow, thieves then would not wish to leave evidence of their gristly work (however, as is their wont, when snow IS falling adequately to cover footprints and wagon tracks, Resurrection-Men will go about their tasks). Laban was in the process of exiting church this Sabbath morn, when a person stated that "a Waggon was heard to pass a House near the grave yard between Midnight & 2 O-Clock."[17] No one thought any harm. It was said the wagon bench held two young men. But to think on it, a woman dressed in white was seated between them. Smith, who was venturing over to pray beside Bathsheba, raced to her slumbering place. His eyes grasped a horror that can not be expressed, he could plainly see that the small stones he'd arranged on the grave had been disturbed. About the mound, muddied straw was strewn. The distraught father placed clenched knuckles beside his temples, and ran for assistance. Neighbors and relations responded at once with shovels and the terrible digging commenced. Simeon Fitch, a cousin to Bathsheba, and William Kimberly and Sidney Painter participated in the retched business.[18] Furious spade-fulls quickly cleared a few feet of dirt when a mournful wail went up. The burrowing paused. Before the group of men lay the favorite tortoise-shell comb Bathsheba wore in life and took with her as a hair-adornment to the Grave. Dear nephew, in a short space of time the coffin was found. It had been split open, some reported that a log had been substituted for the body (but why, I do not know, unless the frail corpse had been stolen prior to interment, but I do digress). Pitiful cries transformed to avenging oaths, while standing beside this fresh hole the men contemplated clues.

A country-gentleman, I know not from what vicinity, was amongst the enraged crowd. This fellow did share to having helped chase-down grave-robbers a few winters back in the Berkshires.

Squatting nex' the sullied grave he did relate that it seemed Resurrection-Men raided Bathsheba's burial during the dark hours of Saturday night or early Sunday.

This finely attired fellow explained the wherewithal of New England grave robbing, or, as the vulgar would term it, "body-snatching." His narrative is of importance, Nephew, and employs information necessary to extract the culprits. It was explained that the very first step in the Art of grave pilfering is observation, the knowledge of where a new burial has occurred. Noting the precise site during daylight hours (what is the grave's location with thought to the cemetery gate, or perhaps the grave adjoins a large tree) such reminders remove the stumbling

Doctors and students required dead bodies for study during a time when cadaver research was deemed immoral and illegal—thus, the ghoulish trade of stealing freshly interred corpses. New Englanders were vigilant about the sound of shovels or a beam of light that would give away late-night cemetery labors. *Courtesy of the Library of Congress, LC-USZ6-1017.*

toil of a nighttime search. Two men customarily conduct the gruesome business, with a third waiting in the vicinity, out of view, with a wagon. Earth is removed at the head of the coffin, which is discerned by the location of the gravestone (if no stone is yet in place, the direction of the body can be determined by the alignment of the graveyard's other markers). Here a three-foot square of earth is removed, not much loam at all, really. The job is fairly an easy chore, the soil already being loosened. Sometimes, a stone slab will have been placed atop the casket, as a detriment, but determined Resurrection-Men will not be impeded by such a tactic. When the box is finally broken open (in no more than an hour's labor) or bored with an augur (axes and saws make far too much noise), the "Hook" is employed—a ghastly instrument. The iron rod is five feet in length; a large hook on one end, a short t-bar handle on the other. The Hook is placed under the chin of the deceased; then the two men merely tug the victim from out the box and into the dark night. The Hook (I beg your pardon at speaking of the device) wretchedly maims the poor person. The group leaning forward to hear this person's narrative became silent.

The Berkshire gentleman continued a moment later, after pausing to mop his brow. Obviously, no chart had been created mapping the grave-top. Otherwise, the stones arranged there by Mr. Smith would have been carefully replaced. Neither was a tarp employed to collect the dirt (and straw) to be poured back into the small hole; this left damning evidence of tampering. This job was sloppy. A second tarp was not used, the custom being to tightly wrap the body so as to leave no evidence (such as the hair-comb). That particular broadcloth lends to another brute name for those in the grave robbing business: sack 'em-ups. As One, the knot of men shouted, "Who would commit their soul to hell with such a vile act?" The gentleman was a bit surprised, saying, "Why, graves, usually of the poor, are robbed all across New England and the city of Manhattan during Autumn and Winter months. That's when Medical schools conduct anatomy lectures. Yale school is not far away."

Following a hush, someone in the cemetery throng called-out a name: Ephraim Colburn. The young man crying at Bathsheba's funeral. Colburn was an assistant at the college.

Let me rest my pen here, and with heavy Heart prepare you for my next letter—a large Mob of angry West Haven men are marching on New Haven this very moment. They should arrive at their destination by day-break.

Yr. Greatly Worried UNCLE,
Mathus

Monday, January 12th, 1824
Nephew—

The devil's claws have New Haven by the Throat. I joined the procession advancing on the town, hoping to gather answers at the Medical College. With Laban Smith in charge, we first sought the advice of General Dennis Kimberly. As you know, he resides in West Haven and practices Law in New Haven (the distinguished fellow also once oversaw the New Haven Grays, our local militia). The crowd was at a terrible loss of what to do, and demanded a search warrant be procured to enable an immediate tumbling of the school's rooms. Shocked with the news of the grave robbery, the good General thought this approach prudent and dutifully complied. Erastus Osborn, our Village constable, whom you certainly recall, will carry out the order. With the signed Warrant in hand, General Kimberly and Constable Osborn went directly to Doc[r]. Jonathan Knight's home at 90 Church Street. This fine surgeon-professor is one of the founders of the M. College. The three men proceeded thither to the Medical school, the "Massive, Stuccoed and Whitewashed"[19] mansion atop College Street. Once intended as a hotel and owned by good Mr. Hillhouse, it was soon leased by Yale and prepared for students and faculty. The gowns usually boast of the facility, (a lecture hall is located on the top floor, a dining room, space for a laboratory in the basement and student rooms throughout. Behind the school a botanical garden lies).[20]

The three search[d] the building from top to bottom and emerged through the front doors, quite startled, to view a spectacular and roiling crowd. The Constable shouted that they found nothing out of the ordinary, except as I suppose, usually to be found at such Institutions and I conclude further search would be unavailing. Bathsheba was not located. Shouts went up from the mob demanding exactly what was found. A brace of men moved toward the building's steps, pausing only with General Kimberly's upraised hands. A rumor set racing through the assembly babbled something about four or five bodies being uncovered beneath a coal pile and body-sized alcoves found chiseled into the basement's foundation-walls.

By this time, the street before the building had filled with hundreds of men from throughout New Haven, West Haven, Fair Haven and neighboring towns. The New Haven Grays, our fine militia, under Captain Philip S. Galpin were called out in an attempt to protect the Medical College. The roughly fifty citizen-soldiers arrived quickly, being that their Headquarters are centered at No. 4 Central Row, on Chapel. Their sudden appearance under arms with visibly provided ammunition stunted the noisome crowd

AN

# ADDRESS

DELIVERED AT THE FUNERAL

OF THE

## HON. DENNIS KIMBERLY,

DECEMBER 16, 1862.

BY THE

REV. ELISHA L. CLEAVELAND, D.D.

NEW HAVEN.
BASSETT & BARNETT.
PRINTED BY TUTTLE, MOREHOUSE & TAYLOR.
1863.

momentarily. All the while, Laban Smith refused to be consoled. The grieving father demanded access to the college for himself and a handful of trusted fellows. The crowd bellowed its approval. Doc[r] Knight negotiated with Smith, and five or six men were chosen. I do admit that I was more than a little shocked to be selected. With his walking stick waving wildly side to side, Constable Osborn opened a path and took the lead. As the throng parted for our small group, the Berkshire gentleman (whom we first met at the West Haven graveyard) shouted to Mr. Smith as we proceed up the several steps to the school's front door: "Sir, and sirs, with all care do examine every crack and crevice. Especially the dome atop the building, and turn your eyes upward into each chimney: these are where we found the stolen bodies of our neighbors." The crowd bore sinister eyes into the building. It appeared as if the structure's frame did shudder.

Terrible and sad are the events that followed. Constable Osborn wisely decided to pen his observations, which he shared with me & request[d] I peruse for accuracy. His own words, which I now dourly employ, spare my soul's own search for adequate verbiage. Once inside the college,

> WE determined to be thorough & I [Osborn] took 5 or 6 West Haven and New Haven Men with me & at length in a small low Cellar, we came to a place in the pavement (the Cellar being paved with large flat stones) which look[d] generally like the bottom of the Cellar throughout, but appear[d] to have a trifle of fresh dirt lying scatter[d] about, hardly however discernible. I scratched with the end of my walking stick and the more I examin[d] the more suspicion was created, we soon found the earth appear[d] fresher between the stones & finally took up a large flat stone where we discover[d] a white bundle, apparently a bundle of cloathes. we examin[d] & found a human body doubled up in a heap entirely cover[d] up with the grave cloathes. we took

*Opposite, top*: Originally built as a hotel by James Hillhouse and later acquired by Yale, this building became the university's first medical school when it officially opened its doors in 1813. Being situated across from the Grove Street Cemetery fostered rumors about secret underground passages allowing for the gruesome removal of corpses to be used for medical studies. *Courtesy of Yale University, Harvey Cushing/John Hay Whitney Medical Library.*

*Opposite, bottom*: New Haven attorney Dennis Kimberly was woken by the pounding on his front door early on January 12, 1824. Laban Smith and West Haven citizens demanded access to the Medical Institution of Yale College. Suspicions were roused that stolen corpses were hidden somewhere inside. Attorney Kimberly prepared the search warrant. A member of the New Haven Grays, he would later rise to the rank of major general in the state militia, was twice elected New Haven mayor (he declined the second term) and was the state attorney for New Haven County. Pictured here is the cover of Dennis Kimberly's 1862 funeral address. *Courtesy of the Michael J. Bielawa Collection.*

New Haven Grays. With the unruly crowd growing ever larger and more vociferous, the local militia was summoned by cries and church bells. This photograph shows the Grays gathering on the Green in 1864, just as they assembled in the same area forty years earlier in an attempt to quell the Cadaver Riots. *Courtesy of the Library of Congress, HABS CONN, 5-NEWHA, 51--13.*

> *it out and it was immediately known to be the Body of the young Woman*
> *we was searching for. The Father was present and was almost distracted,*
> *but greatly rejoiced at the discovery. Doc' Knight says he knew nothing of*
> *its being brought to the College or being there at all.*

Here I pause momentarily so as I may stop my pen from shaking with grief.

But back to the Constable's thoughts: "The hole it [the body] was found in was about 3 feet deep and about 2 in diameter— Doc[r] Knight sent home for a sheet & Cap had the face wash[d] & the sheet & Cap put on, and with a great deal of difficulty the Father & others consented to put the Body into a Waggon to remove it to West Haven."

Within the briefest moment, upon emerging from the school's doors and into the day's winter gloom-light, we were seized by the seething commotion filling the street. Cradled in her father's arms, Bathsheba was carried down the steps of the Medical building, where the crowd capitulated to an overpowering silence that foretold Revenge. The ocean of angry men parted for our small committee. We attempted to gain the Green beyond. Osborn writes, "People had collected from West Haven & New Haven about the College, which was kept fasten[d]." The wide-eyed constable added that "it was now about noon

During the War of 1812, New Haven private Philip S. Galpin served in the First Battalion Connecticut Artillery to defend against a possible British attack. Following the conflict, city residents decided to form a separate local militia, the New Haven Grays. When the Cadaver Riots rolled through downtown the roughly thirty-year-old soldier, now captain of the Grays, took a prominent role in thwarting the mob bent on revenge. *Courtesy of the New Haven Museum Photo Archives.*

when the wagon carried Bathsheba down College Street, then down Chapel Street, on to the lower green where crowds of People collected to view it." Bells toll incessantly. Speakers address the crowds urging an attack on the Medical College. Trembling voices in the mass of men pleaded with me, as I struggled through their midst, whether their recently departed loved ones were in the Cellar amongst the alcoves? (Some men plainly raced from the site stating that they would investigate the graves in their own town's burial-yards.) There were Cries and shouts. Vile oaths and wicked pleas. "Tear down the college" and "Death to

Boldly striding among the rioters, Sheriff Charles Pond sought to control the torch-bearing throng arriving from surrounding towns. His intelligent approach to the volatile situation most likely saved a number of lives. For seven months during 1853–54, he served as governor of Connecticut. *Portrait courtesy of the Museum of Connecticut History and David J. DeRubeis, Cody-White Funeral Service.*

the students."[21] I distinctly heard a clutch of Medical students calling out: "YALE! YALE!" rallying those gowns from the Brick Row of college dormitories. A flurry of students with raised pistols and dirks and clubs forced its way kitty-corner from the college grounds and surrounded the medical building. There was much shoving and punching.

Huzzahs rolled beside the town Cannon seized by the incensed mob. Maddened eyes ominously sighted the gaping iron muzzle at the building. The populace was frenzied beyond control. Remarkably, even in this raucous sway of humanity New Haven's Sheriff, Charles Hobby Pond, never once appeared unnerved. In fact, Dear Nephew, I myself standing within this tumult, witnessed the Sheriff orchestrate a master-stroke. No sledgehammer could pacify this crazed mob, so with deep-thought, Sheriff Pond approached one of the most vociferous speech-makers clamoring for attack and merely tapped him on the shoulder, suggesting this fellow was the best candidate to maintain peace. The ploy was a success and the man assisted Sheriff Pond throughout the ensuing hours.

Students, who previously had fought their way through the crowd, now gathered within the building. Leaning an ear toward the structure, one could discern the desperate sounds of the gowns barricading them-selves inside. This stand-off will be a bloody one, as the mob's numbers continue to swell and the militia is greatly outmanned. Several citizens have already been incarcerated due to Rioting.

I understand that a great procession has formed, well behind me, on the lower Green, with torch and tears, escorting Bathsheba on her return trip home to West Haven.

☞ A CARD.—LABAN SMITH, of West-Haven, in Orange, returns his very grateful acknowledgments to the inhabitants of West-Haven, and likewise to the citizens of New-Haven, for the lively and deep interest taken by them in his late peculiar affliction: and for the ready assistance they offered him in recovering the body of his deceased Daughter, when it had been surreptitiously removed from the grave, in which it was deposited on the late New-Years day.
West-Haven, January 15, 1824.

Laban Smith had this acknowledgement printed in local newspapers. This particular "card" appeared in the *Connecticut Herald* on January 20, 1824. *Courtesy of the Connecticut State Library.*

Even standing next to me, Constable Osborn had great difficulty communicating. Shouting into my ear, over the roar of the mob, that "one Man connected with the Medical College as an assistant has just been committed to Jail I understand for contempt of Court in withholding testimony." Perhaps he refers to an inquest held by General Kimberly, but I know not. Writing this letter upon the rough fence-posts at the Green, I am at a grievous loss as how to proceed. I sought Constable Osborn's council, and he palely stated that he was removing himself from the ugly scene: "I intend to keep at home & let the ferment have vent or subside." This is advice I cannot in good conscience follow.

Mathus

Tuesday earliest morn, January 13th, 1824
Nephew—

It is a few minutes passed midnight. What appears destined to happen will soon occur. The church bells have begun to toll again. Citizens heave stones and rough torches at the Medical build. Sometimes a person races forward and swats at the walls with a heavy stick. A multitude mills about the streets. As I look out upon the darkened Green, I plainly hear the clang & clatter

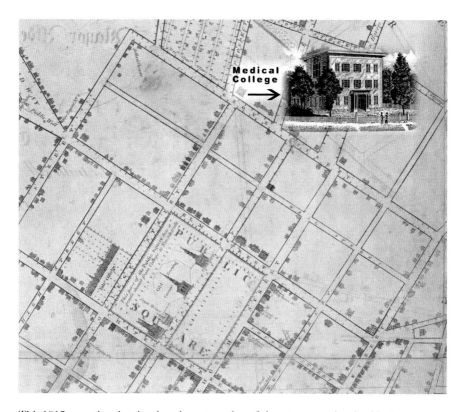

This 1817 map pinpoints just how large a section of downtown was involved in the storming of Yale's medical school. The crowd writhed along College Street from the front of the medical building two blocks deep back to Elm. Another mob assembled on Grove, stretching three blocks east as far as Orange Street. The Green was a third hotspot. The throngs hauled out a cannon and threatened to pulverize the building and kill the students barricaded inside. *Courtesy Library of Congress Geography and Map Division, Digital Id: G3784N Ct002222 Http://Hdl.Loc.Gov/Loc.Gmd/G3784N.Ct002222. Image of Medical Institution at Yale College courtesy of Yale University, Harvey Cushing/John Hay Whitney Medical Library.*

of an Army gathering. Fife & Drum. Silhouettes of a multitude. I hear tell that it is the Governor's Foot Guard. They are determined to bring order to the wild-town. Each soldier equipped with sword and bayoneted rifle, raced to the head of College street at Quick-march; battle drums echo eerily off of the neighboring college Brick Row. The very look of these staunch and resolute soldiers miraculously dispersed much of the madness, whose crazed participants desire no part of their polished and well-practiced weaponry.

M.

## MAYOR'S OFFICE.

### CITY OF NEW-HAVEN, }
### January 16, 1824. }

WHEREAS, on or about the 7th day of instant January, the body of a respectable Female, recently deceased, was unlawfully removed from its place of interment in West-Haven, and brought to this city for dissection :—

Now, therefore, by and with the advice and direction of the Court of Common Council, I hereby offer a Reward of THREE HUNDRED DOLLARS to any person who will discover the offender or offenders, and give such information thereof, that he or they be brought to justice and conviction.

56        GEO. HOADLY, *Mayor*.

New Haven mayor George Hoadley promised a $300 reward for information leading to the arrest and conviction of the person or persons involved with robbing the grave of "a respectable Female recently deceased." Hoadley later also served as mayor of Cleveland. *Courtesy of the Connecticut State Library.*

Tuesday Eve, January 13ᵗʰ, 1824
Dear Neph. Justin—

Bathsheba returned to West Haven this day. A numerous concourse of friends and neighbors stood with Rev. S., whom originally helped lay the delicate child to rest back on New Year's Day. (Once again) he performed the solemn ceremony. The poor girl now resides in her family's garden; certainly a Spring blossom among the Winter weeds. Her grave lies close to a window in her parent's home where she can be lovingly watched-over.

Affectionately Yrs.,
Mathus

February __, 1824
Dear Justin—

Tho anger yet stalks the Green, and stones infrequently pelt the Medical building, New Haven is calm these days. Constable Osborn has related to me, "Two Medical Students have gone off, one of them accused of stealing the Body from the burying ground, as he call[d] upon a Man that has attended the M. College as an assistant since the Lectures commenced to help him conceal it [poor Bathsheba] where we found it." Osborn's mood darkened. During the initial Inquiry "this Man had a hair breadth escape from tarring & feathering by people collected about the County House while the Court of enquiry was proceeding in examining Witnesses—a Kettle of Hatters size & a bag of feathers were in the hands of men at the door & he was just going out when he found he was expos[d] & retreated into the back part of the House—he has since been bound over for trial in $1000 Bond with surety to answer the charge of taking up the Body, as it is suspected he assisted the Student who has absconded."[22]

Allow me to enclose a news-paper article from the *Connecticut Courant* of Feb[y] 17th relaying the outcome of that cur Colburn, may he burn in Hell:

> *During the January session of the Superior Court, held in New Haven, Judge Bristol presiding—Ephraim Colburn was tried and found guilty by the jury, for aiding and assisting in opening the grave and removing the body of a female from the burying ground in Orange, for the purpose of dissection; and was sentenced to nine months imprisonment in the County jail, and to pay a fine of 300 dollars.*

UNCLE MATHUS

# POSTMORTEM

A few months after the trial of the *People v. Ephraim Colburn*, the Connecticut legislature enacted a body-snatching law. The dastardly commission of grave robbing would now be considered a serious crime. More importantly, from the viewpoint of Nutmeg State medical institutions, cadavers would now be supplied by those dying in jail, as well as in the lifeless forms of executed prisoners. This law predated Britain's similar Anatomy Act by eight years.

Poor Bathsheba's name, once associated with a riotous insurrection, speaks quietly to passerbys from the West Haven cemetery where she first, and later finally, found peace. *Photograph by Michael J. Bielawa.*

American dissection riots were not uncommon. Medical schools in Baltimore and Philadelphia experienced attacks. New York's "Doctors' Mob" during the winter of 1788–89 resulted in at least seven killed and numerous injured. Lurid tales of body snatching persistently haunted New Haven well passed the weeklong dissection riots of 1824. Being that the Yale Medical College was located across from the Grove Street Cemetery, rumors circulated that freshly buried bodies were readily supplied through a secret underground tunnel running between the graveyard and the school. Such stories lost popularity when the Medical College moved to York Street in 1860.

(NOTE: events, places, dates and personages herein mentioned are factual. Few liberties have been taken in bringing this tale to light, and those, merely to move the narrative forward. Every quotation is derived from a historical source. Particularly helpful, beyond contemporary newspaper accounts, were Jerome B. Lucke's *History of the New Haven Grays* [1876]; Henry Peck's 1889 history, *New Haven State House with Some Account of The*

*Green*; and especially Hannibal Hamlin's 1935 essay, "The Dissection Riot of 1824 and the Connecticut Anatomical Law." More recent writings include "Anatomy of an Insurrection" by Rachel Engers [2002], featuring wonderful illustrations by Ken Perkins. Specifics to the gruesome history and methodology of body snatching can be found in, "Grave Robbing in New England" by Dr. Frederick C. Waite [1945] and J.B. Bailey's *Diary of a Resurrectionist* [1896]. Yale's earliest medical institution is documented in, "The Medical Institution of Yale College, 1810–1885" by Whitfield J. Bell Jr. [1960] and Harold Saxton Burr's "The Founding of the Medical Institution of Yale College" [1934], both of which appear in the *Yale Journal of Biology and Medicine*. All of Constable Erastus Osborn's words are taken directly from letters he wrote to his father, Shadrack, the postmaster of Southbury, Connecticut, concerning New Haven's dissection riot and are dated January 12 and January 19, 1824. The names of the author and recipient of this chapter's correspondence, that is, between Uncle and Nephew, are a celebration of my brother Matthew [really, nicknamed Mathus] and Justin, my son, who are both a constant fountain of good horror.)

# Notes

## CHAPTER 1

1. Samuel Sly went to live in, or on the grounds near, the Stratford Lighthouse, where he sought work. A falling out with the light keeper found Sly residing farther inland atop Great Hill near the Naugatuck River. He returned to the banks of Long Island Sound and stayed at Captain Nicholl's house in Lordship, Connecticut, before moving to New Haven.

## CHAPTER 3

2. During 1813–14, President Timothy Dwight provided senior class lectures twice a week. The series was extremely popular and addressed a number of exciting topics. On March 23, 1814, he shared, among other supernatural examples, this New Haven story. It is here quoted in its entirety:

> *a respectable inhabitant of this town some years ago, with whom I was acquainted* [furnished the following evidence of spectral visitors]...*At the age of sixteen, and while an apprentice to his father, who was a blacksmith,* [the young man] *was proceeding from a friend's to his father's house at about two o'clock at night, when he saw a person walking at no great distance before him. He took him for a fellow apprentice, with whom, he was on terms of intimacy and warm friendship, and walked to*

*overtake him, making as little noise as possible, intending to take him by surprise. They were but a little distance from the old burying ground on the Green as he drew near, and the course taken by the young man was by one of the paths leading into it. He soon overtook him, and suddenly, extending his arms endeavored to clasp him round the body: but to his surprise, he did not arrest his progress, nor appear to attract his notice, nor was he sensible of feeling any thing in his grasp. Still he was not at all alarmed, but felt so confident that the young man was his friend, that he continued to pursue him, until he proceeded to a spot in the burying-ground, where he stopped and speedily vanished. He thought the occurrence so extraordinary, that he determined to mark the spot, and gathering a few bones, brush and stones together, made a little heap, and proceeded homeward. He went to his room, and retired to bed; after which he learnt from some of the family that his fellow apprentice was sick. His disease which was the pleurisy, soon terminated his life. When the sexton went to the grave-yard, some of the friends, who accompanied him to determine the spot where the grave should be made, without any knowledge of the story of the apparition, chose the place where it had disappeared; so that the first thing the sexton did was to clear away with his spade the little heap by which it had been distinguished.*

3. In addition to the legend of Woolsey Hall's beautiful and possessed organ (see Holzer, "Haunted Organ."), another ghost supposedly inhabits Yale property. In 1900 the "millionaire reverend" Anson Phelps Stokes Jr. (1874–1958) accepted the dual posts as assistant rector of St. Paul's Episcopal Church and secretary of Yale. Moving to New Haven, he sought a quiet antique home and decided on the recently abandoned Pierpont Property. Stokes had fallen in love with the place a few years earlier, while studying at Yale. Built in 1767 by John Pierpont, a grandson of one of Yale's founders, the home had remained in the Pierpont clan from the time it was constructed up until the recent death of a family descendent, eighty-three-year-old Caroline Foster. During Reverend Stokes's initial walk-through, he asked the seller about dark stains saturating the wide plank floors. "Blood," was the reply. The British military had occupied the house during their 1779 invasion of New Haven (prompted in part by Yale's vocal support of the revolution), and the king's troops had converted these rooms into a temporary field hospital. A problem arose during Stokes's attempt to purchase the place; it was discovered that no deed existed for the home, the land being originally acquired by James Pierpont (one of Yale's founders) directly from the local indigenous peoples. Another thorn

developed after Stokes paid his money—he discovered the place was haunted; however Stokes rather enjoyed the romance of the thing. The reverend was told that once every eighty years, and only to the sound of wedding bells, a girl appears in the attic. Dressed in a white muslin dress, her coif dating from the colonial era, she glides silently down each flight of stairs. Her pretty cobwebbed face might be seen staring out from the wavy panes. Proceeding to the backdoor, the delicate ghost enters the courtyard, milling amid the beebalm and mayapple before mysteriously dematerializing.

Since being acquired by Stokes, this home at 149 Elm Street has remained in university hands. It has offered cozy lodgings as a faculty club and later served as the undergradute admissions office. In 1995, it was converted into the Mead Visitor Center for Yale. Any strange occurrences in the building may have a different sort of otherworldly or anthropological explanation. On April 19, 2013, upon examining a series of old photos on display in the visitors' center (portraying the home's early twentieth-century interior rooms) one print clearly shows, off in the corner, a hirsute collection of shrunken heads.

4. The official expulsion document of Louis Fassitt reads as follows:

> *At a meeting of the Faculty of*
> *Yale College, Oct 5th 1843;*
>    *Whereas it is proved to this Board, that Louis Fassitt, a member of the Sophomore class, on Saturday evening of last week, was guilty of wounding, with a deadly weapon, the person of one of the Officers of this college, it is therefore decided and determined, that said Fassitt be, and he hereby is expelled.*
>    *Jeremiah Day*
>    [Yale President 1817–1846]

# CHAPTER 4

5. Godbeer, *Devil's Dominion*, 56.
6. Augur, *Family History*, 9. The title "Dr." was not used by physicians during this era, nor was Mr., except in cases of high respect "accorded only to elders, magistrates, teachers, merchants, men of wealth, etc."
7. Dexter, "At a Court," 58.

8. Hall, *Witch-Hunting*, 73.
9. Thoms, "Beginnings," 319.
10. Personal interview with Lieutenant Christopher Billiau, November 23, 2012. This United States Coast Guard official ascertains that during the season when Howe left Boston the second time, a Canadian high, an atmospheric high-pressure center, could have settled off Nova Scotia pulling a tropical depression from the south. However, Lieutenant Billiau concludes that the severity of the maelstrom gives evidence that Howe had encountered a hurricane.
11. It may have been some of these very same uncaring New Englanders who purposefully marooned Native Americans on Deer Island and Long Island in Boston Harbor. While King Phillip's War raged across New England's colonies from 1675 to 1676, Massachusetts citizens herded Indians onto barges and left them stranded in a much worse situation than even Howe experienced. Deprived of food or shelter, many of these tortured indigenous peoples perished well within site of the Massachusetts shoreline, just about the same time as Howe's misfortunes.

# CHAPTER 5

12. Henry Collins Flagg was born in South Carolina in 1790 (or 1792). Graduating from Yale in 1811, he returned to his southern home to practice law. Returning to New Haven in 1817, he purchased the *Connecticut Herald* and ran the newspaper for two years. Flagg again ventured south to practice law until 1833, when Connecticut's healthy climate called. He served as New Haven mayor from 1834 to 1839 and was elected to the state senate in 1835. An old Southern aristocrat, Flagg practiced with foils on a daily basis, continually on guard to duel for his honor. Flagg's various sage newspaper observations in the *Connecticut Herald—Essays from the Counter of Jeremy Broadcloth, Shopkeeper, Chapel St., New Haven*—were collated and published in Boston in 1822. The editor-mayor died in 1863, a year after his oldest son, Henry (USN commander and artist) passed away.
13. In addition to East Rock, New Haven's neighboring ridges also shared their craggy abodes with hermits. On the southern face of Pine Rock in Hamden, Connecticut (near today's Southern Connecticut State University campus), there once existed "Fry's Cave." The rock shelter was formed by seashore waves during the last ice age. It was named after the Fry family, who for several years resided within the rock overhang, scratching out an existence by

gardening and accepting visitors' alms. In 1826, the Fry family vacated the cave, and a married couple, named Clo and Mac McDaniel, took possession of it. Clo and Mac lived there for about a year, selling the baskets they wove, until the husband's death. Decades afterward, ninety-two-year-old Rhoda Wolcutt of Dixwell Avenue fondly recounted her visits during the early 1830s to the McDaniels's home. The little girl delivered fresh game that her father had hunted to the old African American couple. Rhoda looked forward to hearing Mac's stories and enjoyed keeping the crippled man company while Clo completed errands in town. Within the cave, behind a manmade stone and dirt front, was assembled a wooden "board floor, cupboard, two or three chairs, and a table; but there was no stove, only a rude fireplace with stones for andirons, and no chimney" (the history of the Pine Rock cave is detailed in MacCurdy, "Passing," 511–22.) Another husband and wife moved into the cave and stayed for some time after the McDaniels vacated it; the last occupant, known as Indian George, lived there until 1856. Quarry operations that acquired the site prior to World War I eventually destroyed the trap-rock shelter. During late 1912, extensive blasting resulted in an unplanned, late-night landslide that obliterated the cave and also crushed a nearby agricultural business, killing a large amount of swine. Fortunately, a number of Native American artifacts had been gathered by Yale faculty over the previous few weeks. In addition, coins were unearthed, including a King George penny from 1754 (or 1784), a second English coin dated 1787, a U.S. penny from 1802 and another from 1812. A stone slab was removed that had been inscribed with names of those visiting the cave during the 1750s.

## C<small>HAPTER</small> 7

14. The lighthouse was automated in 1953.
15. Oyster police were responsible for maintaining peace on the oyster beds. They also prevented poaching and other forms of illegal harvest.

## C<small>HAPTER</small> 9

16. Bell, "Medical Institution," 172.
17. Hamlin, "Dissection Riot," 278. Erastus Osborn letter dated January 12, 1824.
18. Peck, *New Haven*, 119.

19. Atwater, *History of the City of New Haven*, 268.
20. Bell, "Medical Institution," 171.
21. Wang, "A Grave Offense," November 1, 2005; Burrow, *History*, 26.
22. Hamlin, "Dissection Riot," 284. Erastus Osborn letter dated January 19, 1824.

# Bibliography

## ARTICLES

"Alarming Delusion." *Churchman's Monthly Magazine* (January 1856).

Beinfield, Malcolm Sydney. "The Early New England Doctor: An Adaptation to a Provincial Environment." *Yale Journal of Biology and Medicine* 15, no. 2 (December 1942).

Bell, Whitfield J., Jr. "The Medical Institution of Yale College, 1810–1885." *Yale Journal of Biology and Medicine* 33, no. 3 (December 1960).

"The Blighted Heart." *Graham's Lady's and Gentleman's Magazine* 23, no. 1 (July 1843).

Brody, Lisa R. "Yale College in the 19th Century: An Archaeological Perspective." *Bulletin of the Archaeological Society of Connecticut* 56 (1993).

Burr, Harold Saxton. "The Founding of the Medical Institution of Yale College." *Yale Journal of Biology and Medicine* 6, no. 3 (January 1934).

Engers, Rachel. "Anatomy of an Insurrection." *Yale Medicine: Alumni Bulletin of the Yale University School of Medicine* 36, no. 3 (Spring 2000).

Frank, Julia Bess. "Body Snatching: A Grave Medical Problem." *Yale Journal of Biology and Medicine* 49, no. 4 (September 1976).

Guest, Raechel. "Myriad of Factories Led to the Collapse of Brass Production in Waterbury." *Waterbury Observer*, February 29, 2012.

Hamlin, Hannibal. "The Dissection Riot of 1824 and the Connecticut Anatomical Law." *Yale Journal of Biology and Medicine* 7, no. 4 (March 1935).

Harrison, Timothy. "Sakonnet Lighthouse to be Restored." *Lighthouse Digest* (January/February 2010).

"Information—We Should Like to Be Informed Why It Is That Light Appears Every Monday Night in the Garret of North Middle." *Yale Courant*, March 13, 1867. (Date on front page incorrectly states February 13, 1867.)

"Is North Middle Haunted?" *Yale Literary Magazine* 34, no. 1 (October 1870).

"Life of New Haven–Born Pirate, Delaney, Ended on the Gallows." *Shanachie.* 3 no. 2 (March–April 1991).

MacCurdy, George Grant. "The Passing of a Connecticut Rock Shelter." *American Journal of Science* (December 1914).

"Murder of New Haven Man, Czar's Former Agent, Stirs America, England and Russia." *Hartford Courant*, August 15, 1920.

"New Haven Sleuths Suspect IWW Hand in Sokolowsky Case." *Hartford Courant*, August 9, 1920.

"The New Haven Tragedy—Witchcraft and Fanaticism—Their Results." *Frank Leslie's Illustrated Newspaper*, January 12, 1856: 72–3.

"North Middle Relics, Tearing Down the Old Dormitory." *New Haven Evening Register*, July 20, 1894.

"North Middle's Doom, Where Noted Men Once Lived." *New Haven Evening Register*, July 16, 1894.

"Parker Hall: 'The Lone Skipper.'" *Duxbury* [MA] *Clipper Anniversary Issue*, May 8, 1975.

"The Shipwreck of Capt. Ephraim Howe." *Essex Antiquarian* 2, no. 12 (December 1898).

"Some Lone Skippers." *Forest and Stream: A Weekly Journal of Outdoor Life* (September 17, 1910).

Thoms, Herbert. "The Beginnings of Medical Practice in New Haven County." *Yale Journal of Biology and Medicine* 6, no. 3 (January 1934).

Trout Amy L., and Julie Ponessa Salathé. "A Brief Introduction to the Maritime History of New Haven." *Journal of the New Haven Colony Historical Society* 37, no. 1 (Fall 1990).

Waite, Dr. Frederick C. "Grave Robbing in New England." *Bulletin of the Medical Library Association* 33, no. 3 (July 1945).

"A Wakemanite—Double Murder." *Frank Leslie's Illustrated Newspaper*, January 12, 1856: 72–3.

Wang, Ivy. "A Grave Offense." *New Journal: The Magazine About Yale and New Haven* (November 1, 2005).

"Wide-Spread Story Had Sokolowsky As Labor Spy While Conflicting Tales Have Wife Working With Striker Lover In Executing Grim Murder Plan." *Bridgeport* [Sunday] *Herald*, July 4, 1920.

"Yale College." *Scribner's Monthly* 11, no. 6 (April 1876).

# BOOKS

Adams, John Turvill. "The Hermit of East Rock." *Poems of John Turvill Adams*. New Haven: A.H. Maltby & Co., 1825. Adams (1805–1882) was a Connecticut newspaper editor, poet and novelist.

Atwater, Edward E., ed. *History of the City of New Haven to the Present Time.* New York: W.W. Munsell & Co., 1887.

———. *History of the Colony of New Haven to Its Absorption Into Connecticut.* New Haven, CT: Printed for the author, 1881.

Augur, Edwin Prosper. *Family History and Genealogy of the Descendants of Robert Augur of New Haven Colony.* Middletown, CT: Press of Pelton & King, 1904.

Bailey, James Blake. *The Diary of a Resurrectionist, 1811–1812: to Which are Added an Account of the Resurrection Men in London and a Short History of the Passing of the Anatomy Act.* London: Swan Sonnenschein & Company, 1896.

Barber, John Warner. *Connecticut Historical Collections.* New Haven, CT: John W. Barber, 1836.

———. *History and Antiquities of New Haven, From Its Earliest Settlement to the Present Time.* New Haven, CT: J.W. Barber, 1831.

Blake, Henry T. *Chronicles of New Haven Green: From 1638 to 1862.* New Haven, CT: Tuttle, Morehouse & Taylor Press, 1898.

Brainard, Ellen, Carol Cooper, Betsy Liapunov, and Lise Orville, eds. *Exploring East Rock.* New Haven, CT: East Rock Neighborhood Association, 1974.

Bremer, Francis J. *Building a New Jerusalem: John Davenport, a Puritan in Three Worlds.* New Haven, CT: Yale University Press, 2012.

"Brief Memoir of John Breed Dwight." *New Englander Vol. IV–1846.* New Haven, CT: B.L. Hamlen, 1846.

Buckingham, Joseph T., ed. *Miscellanies Selected From the Public Journals.* Vol. 1. Boston, MA: Joseph T. Buckingham, 1822. Includes the essays of Henry Collins Flagg.

Burrow, Gerald N. *A History of Yale's School of Medicine: Passing Torches to Others.* New Haven, CT: Yale University, 2002.

Carlisle, Robert J., MD, ed. *An Account of Bellevue Hospital with a Catalogue of the Medical and Surgical Staff From 1736 to 1894.* New York: Society of the Alumni of Bellevue Hospital, 1893.

*Catalogue of the Alumni of the Medical Department of the University of Pennsylvania 1765–1877.* Philadelphia, PA: Society of the Alumni of the Medical Department, 1877.

Clark, George L. *A History of Connecticut, Its People and Institutions.* New York: G.P. Putnam's Sons, 1914.

Daniels, J.W. *Spiritualism Versus Christianity; Or, Spiritualism Thoroughly Exposed.* New York: Miller, Orton & Mulligan, 1856.

Decrow, W.E. *Yale and "The City of Elms."* Boston, MA: W.E. Decrow, 1882.

Dexter, Franklin Bowditch. "At a Court Held in New Haven, February YE 4th 1650." *Ancient Town Records Volume I: New Haven Town Records 1649–1662.* New Haven, CT: New Haven Colony Historical Society, 1917.

————. *Biographical Sketches of the Graduates of Yale College Vol. VI: September, 1805–September, 1815.* New Haven, CT: Yale University Press, 1912.

Dwight, Theodore. *President Timothy Dwight's Decisions of Questions Discussed by The Senior Class in Yale College, in 1813 and 1814.* New York: Jonathan Leavitt, 1833.

Ellms, Charles. *The Pirates Own Book; Or, Authentic Narratives of the Lives, Exploits, and Executions of the Most Celebrated Sea Robbers.* Portland, ME: Sanborn & Carter, 1837.

Flagg, Ernest. *Genealogical Notes on the Founding of New England—My Ancestors Part in the Undertaking.* Hartford, CT: self-published, 1926.

Foote, John P. *Memoirs of the Life of Samuel Foote.* Cincinnati, OH: Robert Clark & Co., 1860.

Fornell, Earl Wesley. *The Unhappy Medium: Spiritualism and the Life of Margret Fox.* Austin: University of Texas Press, 1964.

Glanvill, Joseph. *Saducismus triumphatus; Or, a Full and Plain Evidence, Concerning Witches and Apparitions.* London: n.p., 1681.

Glazier, Captain Willard. *Peculiarities of American Cities.* Philadelphia, PA: Hubbard Brothers, 1886.

Godbeer, Richard. *The Devil's Dominion: Magic and Religion in Early New England.* Cambridge, UK: Cambridge University Press, 1992.

Goodwin, William. *Death Cell Scenes, Or Notes, Sketches and Momorandums* [sic] *of the Last Sixteen Days and Last Night of Henry Leander Foote...Also that of James McCaffrey, for the Murder of Ann Smith.* New Haven, CT: J.H. Benham, 1850.

Gordon, William R. *A Three-Fold Test of Modern Spiritualism.* New York: Charles Scribner, 1856.

Green, J.H. *Twelve Days in the Tombs; Or, A Sketch of the Last Eight Years of the Reformed Gambler's Life.* New York: T.W. Strong, 1851.

Hall, David D. *Witch-Hunting in Seventeenth-Century New England: A Documentary History, 1638–1693.* Boston, MA: Northeastern University Press, 1999.

Hartley, Rachel M. *The History of Hamden Connecticut 1786–1936.* New Haven, CT: Quinnipiack Press, 1943.

Holzer, Hans. *Ghosts of New England.* New York: Wings Books, 1997.

James, Isaac. "The Sufferings of Mr. Ephraim How, of New Haven." *Providence Displayed; Or, The Remarkable Adventures of Alexander Selkirk...A Supplement, Containing the History of Peter Serrano, Ephraim How, and Others, Left in Similar Situations.* Bristol, UK: Biggs and Cottle, 1800.

Leavitt, John F. *Wake of the Coasters.* Middletown, CT: Wesleyan University Press, 1970.

Lewis, Alonzo. *The History of Lynn, Including Nahant.* Boston, MA: Samuel N. Dickinson, 1844.

Lucke, Jerome B. *History of the New Haven Grays*. New Haven, CT: Tuttle, Morehouse & Taylor Press, 1876.

Mather, Cotton. *Magnalia Christi Americana; Or, The Ecclesiastical History of New England*. Hartford, CT: Silas Andrus & Son, 1853.

Mather, Increase. *Remarkable Providences Illustrative of the Earlier Days of American Colonisation*. London: Reeves and Turner, 1890.

Mead, Spencer P. *Ye Historie of ye Town of Greenwich*. New York: Knickerbocker Press, 1911.

Orville, Lise, Carol Cooper, Betsy Liapunov, and Susan Smith, eds. *East Rock Park*. New Haven, CT: East Rock Neighborhood Association, 1972.

Paine, Ralph D. *Lost Ships and Lonely Seas*. New York: Century Co., 1921.

Peck, Henry. *The New Haven State House with Some Account of The Green*. New Haven, CT: Henry Peck and George H. Coe, 1889.

*Poor Mary Stannard! A Full and Thrilling Story of the Circumstances Connected With Her Murder. History of the Monstrous Crime. The Most Mysterious of All the Cases Which Have Baptized Connecticut in Blood. The Only True and Reliable Account. The Clairvoyant's Wonderful Story*. New Haven, CT: Stafford Printing, 1879.

Rawlinson, George. *Ancient History*. World's Greatest Classics. Edited by Julian Hawthorne. New York: Colonial Press, 1900.

Rockey, J.L., ed. *History of New Haven County, Connecticut*. Vol. 2. New York: W.W. Preston & Co., 1892.

Shumway, Floyd, and Richard Hegel, eds. *New Haven: An Illustrated History*. Woodland Hills, CA: Windsor Publications, 1981.

"The Sufferings of Ephraim How." *The Mariner's Chronicle: Containing Narratives of the Most Remarkable Disasters at Sea, Such as Shipwrecks, Storms, Fires, and Famines*...New Haven, CT: George W. Gorton, 1834.

"The Sufferings of Ephraim How." *Remarkable Shipwrecks, A Collection of Interesting Accounts of Naval Disasters…*Hartford, CT: Andrus and Starr, 1813.

"Sufferings of Ephraim How, of New Haven." *The Mariner's Chronicle; Or Interesting Narratives of Shipwrecks.* London: Publisher not listed, 1826.

Tannenbaum, Rebecca. *The Healer's Calling: Women and Medicine in Early New England.* Ithaca: Cornell University Press, 2002.

———. *Health and Wellness in Colonial America.* Santa Barbara, CA: Greenwood, 2012.

Taylor, John M. *The Witchcraft Delusion in Colonial Connecticut 1647–1697.* New York: Grafton Press, 1908.

Trumbull, Benjamin. *A Complete History of Connecticut, Civil and Ecclesiastical.* Vol. 1. New Haven: Maltby, Goldsmith and Co., 1818.

Wakeman, Robert P. *Wakeman Genealogy 1630–1899.* Meriden, CT: Journal Printing Co., 1900.

Waldo, George Curtis. *The Standard's History of Bridgeport.* Bridgeport, CT: The Standard Association, 1897.

## CLIPPINGS FILES

"New Haven's 'Rocks' A Century Ago." *Sunday New Haven Register*, April 17, 1949. New Haven Museum's Dana, Arnold Guyot Manuscript Collection.

"Parker Hall." Clippings File, undated late nineteenth- and early twentieth-century material. Nantucket Historical Association Research Library.

Sandella, Richard. "The Man Who Owned East Rock." *New Haven Register*, October 19, 1984. New Haven Museum's Dana, Arnold Guyot Manuscript Collection.

## CORRESPONDENCE AND INTERVIEWS

"At a Meeting of the Faculty of Yale College, Oct-5th 1843, signed by Jeremiah Day." Letter in "Expulsion of Louis Fassitt, 1843 Oct. 5." Yale College Records Concerning Student Discipline. Yale University Library, Manuscripts and Archives.

Billiau, Lieutenant Christopher. Command duty officer at Sector Long Island Sound. Interview with the author. New Haven, CT, November 23, 2012.

Oldham, Elizabeth. Research associate, Nantucket Historical Association Research Library. Discussions with the author. Nantucket, MA, summer through winter 2012.

Sayle, Charles F. to Edouard A. Stackpole, August 2, 1964. Nantucket Historical Association. Nantucket, MA.


## DIRECTORIES

Benham's New Haven Directory and Annual Advertiser 1853–54 and 1854–55.

"New Haven City Directories." 1840–present. Various publishers including James M. Patton, J.H. Benham and Price and Lee.


## GOVERNMENT DOCUMENTS

*Border Crossings: From Canada to U.S., 1895–1956.* National Archives and Records Administration, Washington D.C. Database online. Ancestry.com Operations, Inc. Provo, UT, 2010.

Hooker, John. *Connecticut Reports: Being Reports of Cases Argued and Determined in the Supreme Court of Errors of the State of Connecticut.* Vol. 30. New York: Banks & Brothers, 1876.

"Niles Nelson." U.S. Coast Guard Awards. *U.S. Department of Homeland Security, United States Coast Guard.* www.uscg.mil/history/awards/GoldLSM/24JUL1903.asp (accessed August 14, 2012).

*Reports of Some of the Criminal Cases on Primary Hearing, Before Richard Vaux, Recorder of the City of Philadelphia.* Philadelphia, PA: T. & J.W. Johnson, 1846.

*Thirty-Seventh Annual List of Merchant Vessels of the United States.* Washington, D.C.: Government Printing Office, 1905.

*Twenty-Sixth Annual List of Merchant Vessels of the United States.* Washington, D.C.: Government Printing Office, 1894.

*United States Coast Guard, Station Gurnet, Massachusetts.* USLSS Station #4. Second District. Coast Guard Station # 30.

*United States Federal Census.* 1830–1940

*U.S. Army, Register of Enlistments, 1798–1914.* National Archives and Records Administration, Washington D.C. Database online. Ancestry.com Operations, Inc. Provo, UT, 2007.

*U.S. Marine Corps Muster Rolls, 1798–1892.* National Archives and Records Administration, Washington D.C. Database online. Ancestry.com Operations, Inc. Provo, UT, 2007.

*U.S. Passport Applications, 1795–1925.* National Archives and Records Administration, Washington D.C. Database online. Ancestry.com Operations, Inc. Provo, UT, 2007.

## MAPS AND ATLASES

*Atlas of the City of New Haven, Connecticut.* Philadelphia: G.M. Hopkins, 1888.

Bache, A.D., and F.R. Hassler. *New Haven Harbor…Survey of the Coast of the United States.* Washington D.C., 1846.

Beers, Frederick W. *Atlas of Long Island, New York: From Recent and Actual Surveys and Records.* New York: Beers, Comstock and Cline, 1873.

———. *Atlas of New Haven County Connecticut.* New York: F.W. Beers, A.D. Ellis and G.G. Soule, 1868.

Doolittle, Amos. "Plan of New Haven." New Haven: A. Doolittle, engraver, 1817.

Hartley and Whiteford. *Map of the City of New Haven and Vicinity from Actual Surveys, etc.* Philadelphia: Collins and Clark, 1851.

# NEWSPAPERS

*American Mercury (Hartford)*
*Boston Daily Globe*
*Bridgeport Advertiser and Farmer*
*Bridgeport Daily Standard*
*Bridgeport Herald*
*Bridgeport Post*
*Bridgeport Republican Standard*
*Brooklyn Daily Times*
*Brooklyn Eagle*
*Columbian Centinel* [sic] *American Federalist (Boston)*
*Columbian Register (New Haven)*
*Columbian Weekly Register (New Haven)*
*Connecticut Courant (Hartford)*
*Connecticut Herald (New Haven)*
*Connecticut Labor Press (New Haven)*
*Connecticut Mirror (Hartford)*
*Constitution (Middletown, CT)*
*Corrector (Sag Harbor, Long Island)*
*Daily Atlas (Boston)*
*Daily Picayune (New Orleans)*
*Duxbury Clipper (Duxbury, MA)*
*Hartford Courant*

*Hartford Daily Courant*
*Hempstead Inquirer (Hempstead, Long Island)*
*Litchfield Republican (Litchfield, CT)*
*Long Island Times (Flushing, NY)*
*Long Islander (Huntington, Long Island)*
*Middlesex Gazette (Middletown, CT)*
*Morning Record (Meriden, CT)*
*National Republican (Washington, D.C.)*
*New-Haven Daily Herald*
*New Haven Evening Register*
*New Haven Journal-Courier*
*New Haven Register*
*New London Day*
*New-London Gazette and General Advertiser*
*New York American*
*New York Daily Tribune*
*New York Evening Telegram*
*New York Evening World*
*New York Herald*
*New York Sun*
*New York Times*
*New-York Tribune*
*Newtown Register (Newtown, Long Island)*
*Norwich Courier (Norwich, CT)*
*Pennsylvania Inquirer and National Gazette*
*Philadelphia Gazette and Commercial Intelligencer*
*Philadelphia Inquirer*
*Queens County Sentinel (Hempstead, Long Island)*
*South Side Signal (Babylon, Long Island)*
*Sunday Republican (Waterbury, CT)*
*Times and Hartford Advertiser*
*Washington Times*
*Waterbury American*
*Waterbury Republican*

# WEBSITES

D'Entremont, Jeremy, "Sakonnet Point Light: Little Compton, Rhode Island," *New England Lighthouses: A Virtual Guide.* www.lighthouse.cc/sakonnet/history.html (accessed August 11, 2012).

———. "Southwest Ledge Light: New Haven, Connecticut," *New England Lighthouses: A Virtual Guide.* www.lighthouse.cc/southwestledge/history.html (accessed February 6, 2013).

———. "Sperry Light (Outer Breakwater Light, New Haven Light): New Haven, Connecticut," *New England Lighthouses: A Virtual Guide.* www.lighthouse.cc/sperry/ (accessed June 27, 2012).

Regarding the Yale dissection riots, Constable Erastus Osborn's letters to his father Shadrach can be viewed online through Yale Library at: http://yaleinsight.library.yale.edu/madid/showthumb.aspx?q1=1035&qc1=contains&qf1=subject1&qx=1004.2 (accessed November 2012).

Waterbury Time Machine II: More Vintage Views & Memories of the Brass City. http://www.freewebs.com/waterbury-ct/big3.htm (accessed April and May 2013).

# About the Author

Michael J. Bielawa has authored regional histories and essays addressing such diverse topics as the mysterious creature in Lake Champlain, Bridgeport's crying statue, the bizarre disappearance of a Hartford minor league baseball manager, baseball symbolism in James Joyce's *Ulysses* and the perplexing, no-hitter curse that confronted the New York Mets for a half century. His work *Wicked Bridgeport* was honored with the first-annual New England Paranormal Literary Award. He has served as a guest curator to the Barnum Museum and as a special consultant to the Fairfield Museum and History Center. Bielawa also provides paranormal history–walking tours of downtown Bridgeport, Connecticut.

Visit us at
www.historypress.net

This title is also available as an e-book.